SAM EVERINGHAM

UNDER THE RADAR

TILLAIR AND CHARTAIR IN THE TERRITORY

Stethoscope Publishing
105/2 Clarke St, Crows Nest, NSW 2065 Australia

First published in 2024 by Stethoscope Publishing
2nd edition (2025)

Text © Sam Everingham
Design by BKA+D

All rights reserved

Typeset in Palatino
Printed and bound by Ingram Spark

ISBN 978-0-6455059-7-9

Under The Radar – Tillair & Chartair in the Territory, Everingham, Sam

 A catalogue record for this book is available from the National Library of Australia

CONTENTS

Introduction 5
Roots 9
Fresh meat. 27
Fighting for a charter licence 37
Seizing opportunities. 47
Tillair: the Industry's employer of choice. 55
Thinking for themselves 67
Groote Eylandt and Numbulwar. 79
A maintenance division. 93
Gove. 105
Life and death. 113
Making their mark on Katherine 125
Acquiring Chartair. 137
Near misses, mishaps and a win 149
Ayers Rock 163
New planes and helicopters .179
Staff and regulatory problems 193
Selling up. 205
Back in the industry. 213
Epilogue. 223
Tillair-Chartair Staff 1977 - 1988. 235
From the TILLAIR Album 241
Acknowledgements. 253

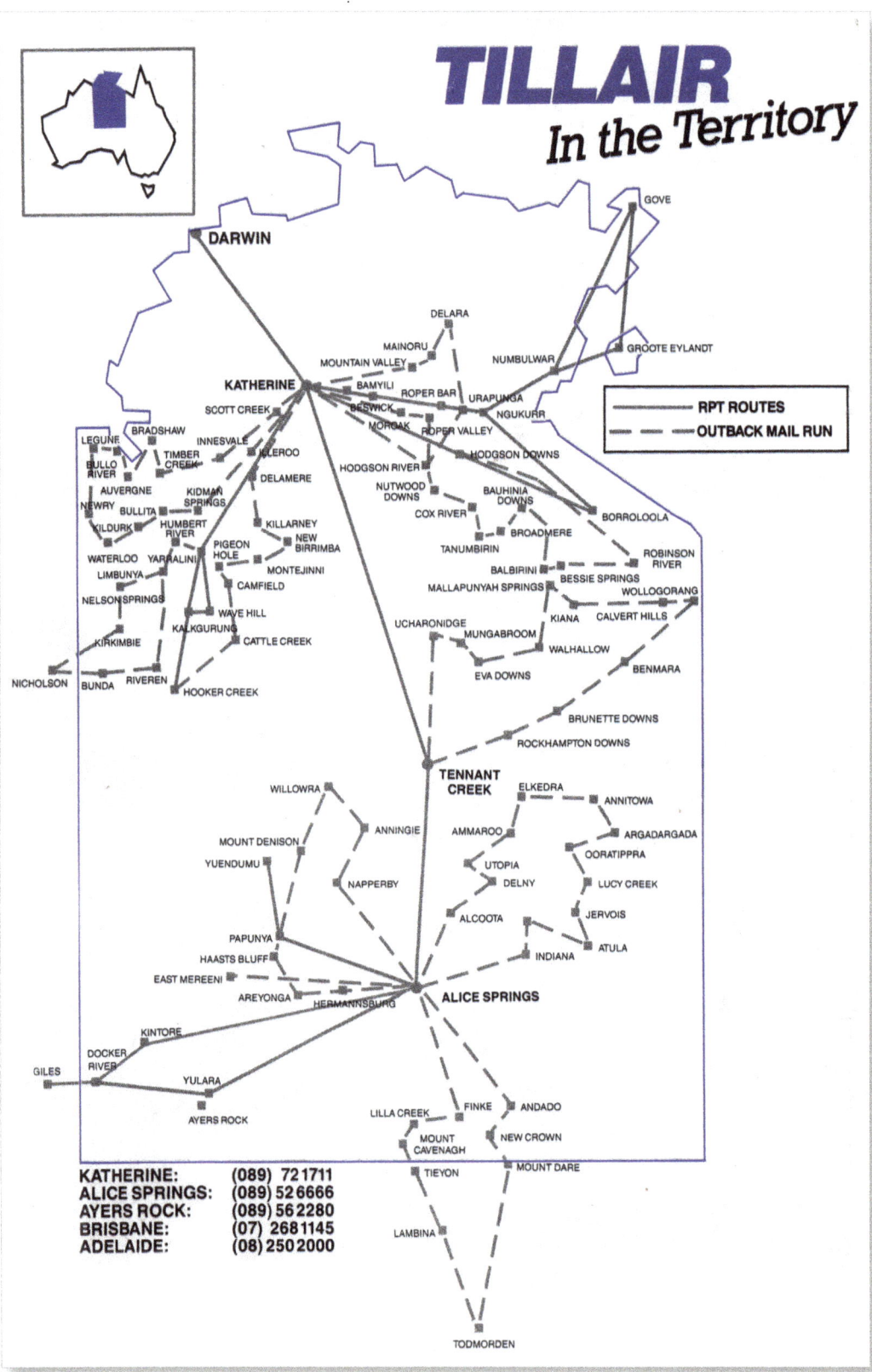

INTRODUCTION

It was the Northern Territory that welcomed Australia's first international aviators back in 1919. Keith and Ross Smith landed in Darwin in December that year in their Vickers Vimy after 28 days and nearly 136 hours flying time from London, to collect their £10,000 prize for the first Australian to fly from England in less than 30 days.

However, no one had warned them about the extreme heat the Territory could muster in the crossing from Darwin to Sydney. The Vimy was forced down at Cobbs Creek in the Territory with a split propeller. In 52°C heat, the mechanics toiled for three days to make repairs, gluing wood splinters into the shattered end and reshaping it using glass from a broken bottle. The Smiths made another unscheduled landing near Charleville when their out-of-balance port engine exploded at 900 metres altitude. This repair alone took 50 days. The crossing from London seemed straightforward compared to crossing the vast Australian outback.

Nonetheless, the Smith brothers' achievement gave the government the confidence to pass the Air Navigation Act in 1920, calling for tenders to undertake mail runs from Sydney to Brisbane, Charleville to Cloncurry and Geraldton to Derby. Darwin also became the launchpad for the first aerial mail link to England, operated jointly by Qantas Empire Airways and Imperial Airways.

As the closest departure point for Europe the Territory made sense, but tackling the harsh interior was another matter. Hudson Fysh's survey of an air route from Darwin to Queensland for the defence department had been shelved back in 1919 given the lack of refuelling or emergency landings options. The vast Northern Territory itself was the last place authorities envisaged air services. For decades, no operator was able to service the vast outback cost effectively. That is, until John Tilley arrived.

This is the story of Tillair and the extraordinary pilots and support staff who went the extra mile to provide one of the outback's most necessary services. In less than ten years this business grew to a fleet of 45 aircraft employing 120 staff: 55 pilots and 65 ground staff. For a time it was the southern hemisphere's largest privately owned airline. Many of the tales in the pages ahead have been so often told and retold over a beer or three that the specific details of who was involved in which incidents have reshaped themselves over time. But logbooks (seldom) lie, and it seems even young pilots retain this written evidence. Tillair was indeed an extraordinary training ground.

ROOTS

In the winter of 1939, John Tilley was born in Adelaide's Memorial Hospital. His childhood was in regional South Australia: Manna Hill, then Terowie and finally Napperby. An only child, John was first schooled at Napperby's tiny one-room school. By the age of nine, like most country kids he knew how to drive a car. When the Napperby school closed he was enrolled at Broad Creek, riding along the cattle track on his push-bike each morning. John failed his Grade 6 subjects and switched to the Solomontown school. It was here that one teacher, a Mr Kean, left a lasting impression on the lad.

John's mother had the confidence to talk to anyone she met. She did not think to introduce herself, but just launched into conversation. It was a trait John inherited. John's senior years were spent at Port Pirie's public high school. He was never a good student and his time there was in the commercial class for those destined for a trade rather than university.

At the age of sixteen he failed the Intermediate Certificate. All he wanted was to drive trucks, and by June 1955 he had a heavy vehicle licence. As soon as it arrived in the mail, John lost no time picking up casual shifts carting lead from the Port Pirie smelting works and taking it down the wharf to load aboard the ships at dock. He borrowed a friend's Maple Leaf 5-tonne truck for the work. The Maple Leaf had no indicator lights; instead, it had a metal arm you adjusted to let the vehicles behind know you were stopping or turning.

Still at school, John used every weekend and holiday to pick up shifts. Port Pirie's booming lead-smelting industry meant regular work and the wages were good.

*

Young John could eke out a humble life or forge his own success. Driven to succeed, he chose the latter. A job in a distinguished company might give him the leg up he yearned for.

In December 1955 he applied as a junior clerk with Elder, Smith & Co., one of South Australia's oldest and most successful pastoral behemoths – a company with a 100- year heritage in the wool-broking business. South Australia had always been its biggest territory, with offices in 56 regional towns. Since its inception, Elders had expanded into offering stock and station agent services as well as financial loans to the pastoral sector around the nation.

John was invited for an interview. In January 1956, Elders head office wrote back. He had the job at a pay rate of £353/12 per annum as well as a £166/8 living away from home allowance. He was instructed to report for duty at Elder's Jamestown branch on the last day of January, before which he was to provide a certificate of health from his local GP. The company had arranged accommodation for the lad in a local boarding house.

> *John's time with Elder, Smith & Co would influence his outlook and life goals immeasurably.*

John's time with Elders would influence his outlook and life goals immeasurably.

In Jamestown, goods deliveries from the train station to the Elders office were made by a horse-drawn trolley. There were regular merchandise and woolpack sales to account for, and you needed to remember to add the tuppence stamp duty to each cash payment receipt. John became adept with an adding machine.

It was here that John gained his first familiarity with a device that would become integral to his very being: the telephone. His first task was ringing graziers to let them know what price their sheep had fetched in the saleyards.

The young man purchased a 350cc BSA motorbike, and each weekend he would ride home to Napperby. Within months Elders had moved him for a temporary assignment in Wirrabara; Elders paid for a hotel room. From Wirrabara he was transferred to Wilmington and then later in 1956 to Tumby Bay. This posting had its own staff quarters, complete with a chip heater, tin bath and wire-sprung bed. John outsourced his washing and ironing, paying a local laundry lady 15 shillings a month. Meals were uncomplicated: a Mars Bar for breakfast. He was finally able to afford a car, investing in a 1951 Holden. At Tumby, all goods arrived by ship, the diesel-powered *Minnipa* run by the Adelaide Steamship Company. Here John was responsible for managing merchandise sales to Elders clients. This included shipping cured, smelly sheepskins back to Adelaide for sale.

By September 1957 John had been moved again, this time to Crystal Brook. Though he had few possessions, Elders always covered the relocation costs. In a boarding house midweek, and travelling to Napperby on weekends, it was here the young lad started to learn about servicing Elders clients during the off-shear sheep sales season.

In January 1958 he was posted to Streaky Bay, a district filling up with soldier settlers not long returned from the world war. Upgrading to a Ford Zephyr, John boarded with a local family and socialised. By now Elders were stocking gas stoves and ovens,

17-year old Tilley purchased his first vehicle - a 350CC BSA motorbike to get around on in 1956

powered by a revolutionary fuel source: portable gas canisters. They became immensely popular.

His 1959 posting was to Peterborough, a big railway hub. John slept in a tiny bedroom out the back of the firm's shopfront office with a chip heater to keep warm. It was here he learned about wool-broking. At the time, Elders, Smith & Co. had the largest share of the Australian wool-broking market. The young man's responsibilities included assisting in yarding and drafting, trucking up to 32,000 merino sheep at a time at the monthly auctions.

'The auctions would often start at 5.00 am,' John recalls. After the sales, 'We sorted the various mobs and loaded them onto railway trucks, depending on what part of the state they needed shipping to their buyers. We might not finish the job until 2.00 am.'

The same year he met Margaret Kennedy, a Peterborough local. When in February 1959 John was posted 500 kilometres south to Bordertown, the pair kept in touch by writing letters. Unable to get home, John's mother sent him a cake for his 21st birthday.

It was in the Bordertown district that John witnessed the transformation of South Australia's Ninety-Mile Desert into productive farmlands. Investors such as the AMP Society took advantage of scientific research that showed that by adding superphosphate and small amounts of copper and zinc to the soil, legume-based pastures could be consistently farmed. For John and the Elders team, this meant a whole new market for selling chemicals, fencing and iron for shearing sheds. By now Tilley was becoming adept at balancing the accounts ledgers each month.

Tilley had developed a reputation as a hard worker and fixer. He was good at sorting out problems

John by now had developed a reputation as a hard worker and fixer. He was good at sorting out problems with accounts, so Elders promoted him to stock salesman in their Pinnaroo office. This promotion came with a company car, an FC Holden ute, and responsibilities for assisting with the buying and selling of stock on behalf of local landholders. On a typical client trip he would begin the day in Pinnaroo in South Australia for breakfast, head to the Yelta sheep sales, followed by lunch in Wentworth, New South

John Tilley & Margaret Kennedy began dating in 1959

Wales and drive home south down the Calder Highway, stopping in Ouyen, Victoria en route for dinner – three states in a day.

In Pinnaroo the young man proposed to Margaret. John sold his beloved Ford Zephyr to put some money aside for a wedding and the pair were married in Margaret's home town of Peterborough on 4 November 1961.

> **In Pinaroo Tilley proposed to Margaret Kennedy.**

*

One of John's clients had bought a local Pinnaroo business, Four Square Store, and needed someone he could trust to manage it. He offered John an annual salary of £1,500 to take on the role. For the newlywed couple this was a huge amount. In March 1962, John resigned from Elders and took the management position. He bought a flash car to celebrate, but the tension between the much older employees and their 22-year-old boss was unbearable. Little more than three months in John re-applied for his Elders job, realising the grass was not always greener on the other side.

Within three weeks Elders agreed to take him back, but he was demoted to a more junior office role in Balaklava, on a salary of £987/4 per year with two weeks annual leave. It was here on 6 November 1962 – Melbourne Cup Day – that Margaret gave birth to their first child, a son they named Scott.

By 1963, Elders had restored John's position as stock salesman, this time in the Coonawarra's Penola branch. The role again came with a car and even a company house for his young family in quiet Kidman Place. It sounded like a simple thing, but for the first time John had home-cooked meals of a night and his laundry could be done at home: nappies, shirts, trousers and underwear all boiled up in a copper.

It was in the Coonawarra district that John had his first thorough introduction to cattle, learning how to draft and value them. The district was also well known for its fat lambs. John looked after all the graziers west of the township.

*

Less than a year after Scott's birth, John recalls Margaret pricking her finger at home with a nappy pin. Strangely, the small wound refused to heal. After a GP visit, she was referred for tests to Royal Adelaide Hospital. When the tests came back, it was John Tilley the doctor wrote to. His letter was short and to the point: Margaret had a blood condition, leukaemia. There was no treatment available. Aged just 25, she had possibly six months to live. Given her youth, the specialist advised John to spare his young wife the truth. 'Go and live life as much as you can together. You need to stay positive for her.'

It did not occur to John to do otherwise. Bearing a ghastly secret, he told only Margaret's parents and his boss. Elders head office lost no time in arranging a transfer for John to Burra in the Bald Hills range, just 90 minutes' drive from Margaret's own family. Once the site of a major copper mine, Burra was by then a pastoral centre. Servicing wealthy graziers whose families had settled in the district generations earlier, Burra had been the state's main sheep-trading centre until the 1950s. From Burra, Tilley might drive out to a drought-stricken Broken Hill with a prospective buyer to inspect sheep. It was in this wealthy district that he made lasting friendships he would maintain for life with men such as Don Stockman. John Tilley dreamed of buying his own grand estate in the district.

> **Within five months, John's young wife, Margaret, was dead and buried in Adelaide's Centennial Park Cemetery.**

Within five months, his young wife was dead and was buried in Adelaide's Centennial Park Cemetery. John needed to return to work. There was no choice but to send his fourteen-month-old infant away to live with Margaret's parents Rita and Jim Kennedy in Peterborough. Scott's first memories are of a woodchip heater and his grandfather's Morris Minor ute.

John blocked out his grief, throwing himself into his work. He and Don Stockman decided a road trip would be a good distraction, so they threw a swag into Don's Valiant ute and drove north, up through western New South Wales to Charleville, where pastoralist Max Bushell had a property. Tilley recalls how stunted in size many of the drought-affected sheep were in this district compared with the large-framed South Australian mobs.

Driving further north through Springsure and Emerald, the pair eventually reached Cairns, returning down the coast road through Brisbane (where Charleville graziers had arranged dates with their daughters) and the sleepy Gold Coast. John was coming to understand the value and quality of pastoral land across the country. What struck the young Tilley was how much potential there was in the wide band of under-valued acacia-wooded grasslands – Brigalow country – between Townsville and Emerald.

*

By the mid-1960s a recession was impacting not only farmers, but Elders' own operations. Smaller regional branches would need to be closed. John was given the management role at the Wirrabara office, in the southern Flinders Ranges, but it was essentially to close the branch and manage the customer fall-out. He was given the same task at the Owen branch, just north of Adelaide.

Finally, John was posted to Elders' head office in Currie Street, Adelaide. Having merged with Goldsborough Mort a

John Tilley (second from left) broking a deal at Burra sheep sales in 1963 with sellers and buyers

few years earlier, the publicly listed behemoth was now paying its shareholders handsome returns each year. John's role was in Elders' land department, driving prospective cashed-up buyers around to view farms in the state's south-east. These were exciting times for land development, with huge swathes of new country being opened up to farming. John soon became adept at spotting opportunities.

It was then that he spent time learning to fly with an air club in Port Pirie. He took lessons and gained a restricted licence. Not long after he graduated, John's flying career came to an abrupt halt. He succeeded in not only writing off the small airplane, but breaking his ankles and collarbone. He refused to ever fly a plane again.

> **It was then that Tilley learnt fly with an air club in Port Pirie and gained a restricted licence.**

Nonetheless, with his good friend Bob Buchanan at the controls, John did take a flying trip in 1966 in a Cessna 172, via Katherine and Darwin to Daly Waters and on to Groote Eylandt. This second adventure took his understanding of the sheer scope and potential of the Australian outback to another level. Though he had no capital to purchase his own station, Tilley could see the outback was being sorely overlooked. There were opportunities to provide services and make money, and he had an uncontrollable urge to be a part of that.

*

By then the man was socialising with friends and clients in Port Pirie on weekends, near to his family's place. John had come to know Port Pirie's local doctors well. One of these, Dr Vern Potter, was interested in land speculation. He and another wealthy local, Brian Condon, who had made his money with the local Moyles soft-drink factory and later Coca-Cola Company, were keen to find ways to minimise their tax. By 1968, Tilley had the answer for them: he had seen with his own eyes the land up around Katherine, a remote community in the Northern Territory of just 1,500 people. Land was cheap but water was plentiful, and there was a place for sale: 10,000 acres with 5 miles of river frontage. The capital development required to turn it into a small cattle property – erecting fencing and cattle yards – was all tax deductible.

'Pandamus' was named after the plentiful palm-like pandanus trees by a bloke who couldn't spell. Potter and Condon bought the land and Tilley helped them form a separate operating company. Elders would not allow him to buy in, declaring it a conflict of interest, so he put the shares in his mother's name.

> For Christmas 1970, Tilley bundled his seven-year-old son Scott and his mother into the car and started on the route north to Katherine.

A manager had been put on to oversee the place, but two years in Potter and Condon suspected the guy was taking advantage. Tilley saw his opportunity: what if he left his city job and ran the Pandamus station? The trouble was that Elders was paying him just $4,000 annually, while the Territory manager's job paid just $1,500 plus food and accommodation. Still, Tilley reckoned he had nothing to lose. If it failed he could return to Elders, but the Territory might be his chance to build something great. It solved the problem for Potter and Condon, so on 30 October 1970 Tilley tendered his resignation from Elders with a month's notice.

For Christmas 1970, Tilley bundled his seven-year-old son Scott and his mother into the car and started on the 2,500 kilometre route north to Katherine. The first 90 kilometres to Port Augusta were bitumen, then the road was dirt to Alice Springs. The three slept in swags beside the vehicle at night, arriving on New Year's Day. Scott and Gwen returned to Napperby after the holidays and Tilley stayed on.

The Tilley family's Katherine home Pandamus, was just a large tin shed with dividers in their early years

The place abutted the Katherine River, looking out to the pretty Donkey Camp waterhole: the home's water supply and swimming hole. The freshwater crocodiles were apparently harmless. The homestead was shared with another couple: Dr Potter's son and young wife had also come up to help out. John would never admit it, but while he could value and trade stock, neither he nor the other bloke knew much about cattle farming.

> **Within months John Tilley was appointed secretary of the Territory's Cattlemen's Association.**

Tilley's new digs were, like most in the Territory, little more than a tin shed, with huge spaces under the walls and eaves to encourage airflow. It was in fact a Sidney Williams hut, of which there were hundreds in the Territory at the time. First appearing at military sites in Darwin and Katherine during the Second World War, these steel-framed implement sheds were corrugated iron clad with ripple-iron double doors at each end. There were no glass windows; instead, double-gauzed push-out shutters along the sides were set alternately high and low to allow airflow with rough curtains. The flexibility allowed the 20-foot sections to be joined. The 60-foot long hut had a verandah at one end that also housed the bathroom.

Tilley promptly threw himself into local community groups, and within months he was appointed secretary of the Territory's Cattlemen's Association. The role came with a small monthly pay cheque, a welcome addition to his meagre manager's allowance.

*

Back at Port Pirie for a break later in 1971, Tilley met someone. Jenny Burdon was eleven years younger at just twenty years old and the daughter of another Port Pirie doctor, Ken Burdon, and his wife Lois, a physiotherapist. Jenny had boarded at Adelaide's Loreto Catholic school, an experience that pushed her to overcome her natural shyness. She had a retail job in Myers Adelaide, returning home on weekends. She recalls meeting John at an Apex Club vintage dinner ball in Port Pirie. Tilley 'was really good-looking', Jenny admits, 'brown skin and dark brown eyes. I picked someone sensible, because I was airy fairy.'

She and John started dating, learning to waterski together on the local waterways. Jenny's parents hosted her lavish 21st birthday in October 1971 at their Port Pirie home, decorating the rooms with king-size, multicoloured daisies. Coloured lights twinkled in the trees throughout the garden. Her parents laid on a smorgasbord of cold platters and a suckling pig in the dining room, followed by dancing. After a toast to his daughter, Dr Burdon announced Jenny's engagement to Tilley.

Soon after, Jenny made the long trip up from Port Pirie to visit by bus. She had been warned ahead what to expect, but the decades-long build up of spider webs in the high-ceilinged structure – too high to reach with a broom – must have been daunting. The young girl hated housework; at least there was a washing machine with a wringer. The floors were rough concrete, 'like a choppy sea', so hard to sweep. The summer heat could be well above 35°C, and pedestal fans were all they had for cooling.

Jenny shrugged. She would adjust.

Returning to Adelaide, Jenny learned to drive in preparation for her move to the outback and began making her wedding dress. The time away from John began to drag. On the phone to Katherine she warned him, 'If we don't get married soon, I'll have to start making a winter wedding dress.'

'I can be down in three weeks,' John countered.

John Tilley married Jenny Burdon in Port Pirie, SA in April 1972

When the pair married in Port Pirie in April 1972, Jenny's family insisted it be in their Catholic church. Just three days later, when others might be honeymooning, John packed his new bride into his XT Falcon station wagon and they made the long road trip to Pandamus via Alice Springs. Again they camped by the side of the road each night in John's swag.

John planned to breed Brahman bulls. The property enjoyed a 5-kilometre frontage onto the river so their herd would never go thirsty, but with another couple in the tiny house and partitions rather than walls dividing the space, there was no privacy.

Tilley had already made a core group of friends, so Jenny quickly felt welcomed in the community. He was soon singing the praises of the district to friends down south. When Katherine needed a new stock agent, Tilley had a suggestion: his close friend and Elders colleague John Dyer from Snowtown. Dyer's wife Val got a job immediately as deputy head at the Katherine school. The couple would go on to buy one of the Territory's iconic stations, Hayfield, halfway between Katherine and Tennant Creek.

Six months after settling in, Dr Potter's son and young wife moved out and Tilley's son Scott moved in, after almost a decade apart. Within days Scott was calling Jenny 'Mum'.

Back at the property, without any air-conditioning John and Jenny instead relied on oscillating electric fans to move the air around. At night in bed they argued about whether the fan should oscillate or stay facing them in bed. Without glass in the windows, each night small fruit bats would encircle their bed as they slept. Swathed in a mosquito net, Jenny would flick the netting each morning to ensure all the bat poo fell off before emerging to face the world.

> *Tilley fattened up Brahman cattle during the wet season then sell them at a profit to much bigger station owners.*

Outside, Jenny wore bathers much of the time. Housecleaning consisted of a pressure hose over the concrete floors. With raised partitions between rooms, it was a simple process.

John and Jenny quickly became close friends with neighbour Maitland Hayes, who everyone called 'Lennie' and sometimes 'Shorty ', and his wife Patsy. Lennie knew and bred cattle: he had

Grahame Heaslip, John Tilley and Jenny Burdon at the latters 21st birthday in October 1971. It was here their engagement was announced.

worked the country for years, jackerooing for the Vesteys on Wave Hill station.

Tilley would fatten up Brahman cattle on Pandamus during the wet season then sell them at a profit to much bigger station owners such as Bill Tapp at Killarney station, but when Arabia's Organization of the Petroleum Exporting Countries, led by Saudi Arabia, proclaimed an oil embargo in late 1973, it sent the price of oil skyrocketing nearly 300 per cent. Triggering a global recession, even in the remote Territory this had a flow-on impact: the price of shipping cattle and meat to distant markets skyrocketed and the local beef industry collapsed. No one could afford to buy John's Brahman stock. 'Our backs were against the wall,' Tilley recalls.

With no market for his stock, Lennie Hayes needed to do something. Before 1960 there had been no abattoirs in Katherine. Back then, cattle had been walked along the Murranji stock route pioneered by drover 'Nat' Buchanan in 1881 to be processed in Queensland's Cloncurry saleyards.

When Katherine opened a meatworks in the 1960s, Territory graziers at last had a market for the thousands of bulls being shot because no one wanted to buy them. The demand was from the USA for lower-quality hamburger beef. Within a few short years, the US was buying $4 million worth from Katherine's meatworks annually. However, by 1970 the Katherine meatworks operation was failing to meet minimum US standards. Katherine lost its export licence, along with Derby, Wyndham and Darwin.

> **Lennie suggested to Tilley: 'Why don't you lease a plane or two, blast freeze our meat the night before and fly it to the mission communities?'**

Lennie wanted to do something different. He had experienced first-hand the ongoing problems stations and communities had in obtaining regular food and supplies, particularly during the wet when access could be cut for months on end. He saw an opportunity. Remote missions had no access to fresh produce; instead, they relied on occasional deliveries of meat by barge from Darwin after it had been shipped from Brisbane. It had often already been frozen for over a year.

Lennie's father-in-law had a set of cattle yards on his place and an old Massey Ferguson 165 tractor. It was enough to set up a makeshift abattoir where, by rigging a bucket onto the front loader along with meat hooks, the slaughtered beasts could be hung and bled out. They erected a small meatworks to chop up the meat and bag it. Their first client were the local grader operators Fraser Henry and Neville Walker.

Lennie was no good with numbers, so he asked John to come on to look after marketing, management and accounts. Though Tilley had no formal training, his years balancing the Elders books had given him comfort with numbers. Soon enough Lennie set up a butcher's shop in Katherine, Uralla Meats, to sell his beef, but he was not interested in overseas export. One night over his favourite tipple – Johnny Walker on ice – Lennie suggested to Tilley: 'Why don't you lease a plane or two, blast freeze our meat the night before and fly it to the mission communities?'

Tilley couldn't help but think Lennie's idea had legs.

Lennie & Patsy Hayes in the late 1970s

FRESH MEAT

Eager for a business opportunity, to Tilley the idea of air freight appealed. Another friend, George Westmacott, was manager at the 2 million-acre Elsey station, then in the hands of a Hong Kong shipping company. Elsey had a Cessna 205 aircraft bought from Bush Pilots Airways in Cairns. George offered to fly Tilley to the remote Milingimbi mission, a community with no road access, to test the idea of fresh meat.

> **George Westmacott offered to fly Tilley to the Milingimbi mission to test his idea.**

The only communication with the place was via an HF radio phone box a quarter mile from the local store. The device had a red light and white light indicator. If the white light was on the operator could be contacted to book a call, but even then it might be another few hours before the call could be put through.

Tilley showed the storekeeper his fresh meat and voiced his proposal. It was a far cry from the one-year deep-frozen variety. 'Forget ringing ahead. We'll bring in a half tonne of meat Tuesdays and Thursdays. At 10 am we'll circle the town. When you hear us, drive out with your van to the airstrip. If you want to change the next meat order – more rump or less or whatever – just tell the pilot.'

*

> **Jenny gave birth on 10 January 1974 to their first child, a daughter Sarah**

Meanwhile, Jenny gave birth on 10 January 1974 to their first child, a daughter Sarah, in Katherine's hospital in the heat of summer. With the family growing, Tilley realised that their rough home needed some renovating: a closed-in room for their infant daughter in particular. Carpentry was required for the build; however, obtaining reliable tradesman in remote Australia was a challenge

John found a bloke, Don Drury, an alcoholic Katherine handyman and carpenter in his fifties. Often Don just failed to turn up for work. Tilley tried picking him up from Katherine each morning but too often, having got on the piss, Don had made out with a local sheila, been knocked out in a fight with locals or was too hungover to be any use. Finally, Tilley realised the only way he could get any work reliably done was to have Drury live at Pandamus, so Scott found himself sharing his bedroom with the guy for months on end. Don would down a bottle of Beenleigh rum daily, but at least he was on site.

Once baby Sarah's room was renovated, it was the only one with floor to ceiling walls. For the first time they could install an air-conditioning unit, at least for one room of the dwelling.

Jenny Tilley remembers she had no money in these early years. She had an account at the chemist and another at the supermarket that John would pay off intermittently from his meagre $100 a week income. Every expense was monitored. They could kill and eat their own beef, so there was no buying chicken from the store as a change. While there were fish in the adjacent river, none of the family were any good with a rod. Jenny recalls Tilley rousing on her when he saw the monthly chemist account included a pack of jellybeans.

> **The couple's second child was born in late January 1976; they named her Penny Louise.**

The couple's second child, another daughter, was born in late January 1976; they named her Penny Louise. Less than four weeks later John's own father, 'Growl', had a fatal heart attack in Napperby.

Until her second child came along, Jenny worked every day on Lennie's Katherine property in the meatworks. John would bundle nine-month-old Sarah into his ute or tractor for the day until Jenny returned. Sarah got used to sleeping in the heat.

Adjacent to the meatworks, Lennie had erected a basic retail shop. There would be four men out front butchering the cattle, while inside Jenny and Patsy Hayes packed the cuts into polystyrene and plastic-wrapped and labelled the meat parcels in preparation for freezing and flying to remote settlements. 'People would come in and yack and we would know all the scandals anywhere in town,' Jenny recalls. 'It's amazing what people will talk about when they don't think anybody's listening . . . It was absolutely hilarious.'

*

John Tilley needed a pilot and an aircraft to make his plans with Lennie a reality. The Baptist mission 550 kilometres away in Hooker Creek had a Cessna and a pilot, Greg Vaughan. They were willing to lease their aircraft, but a charter arrangement could not last. Tilley recalls that with an aircraft that was not his, 'I couldn't guarantee my promise of flying over Milingimbi at 10.00 on Tuesday and 10.00 Thursday because I didn't have control of the aeroplane.'

> **Tilley needed a plane of his own. SA and Territory Air Services (SAATAS) had a second-hand Cessna 206 VH-RCO available for $16,000**

Tilley needed a plane of his own. SA and Territory Air Services (SAATAS), one of the two licensed charter operators in the Territory, had a second-hand six seater Cessna 206 VH-RCO available for $16,000, but with no capital that seemed a tough ask. The Cessna fixed undercarriage attached to the fuselage, so it gave the plane a sturdiness to allow it to handled rough airstrips. This one had a cargo pod beneath the fuselage, so offered an attractive carrying capacity for Tilley's meat deliveries.

All Tilley needed was enough money, and for that he needed to think outside the square. He still had plenty of contacts at Elders, so on 11 November 1975 he took a punt, travelling to Alice Springs to buy 500 young Shorthorn steers at $19 a head from a

local station. The date is etched in Tilley's mind, given it was the same day John Kerr dismissed Prime Minister Gough Whitlam.

Tilley put his speculative stock on agistment for a few months at a nearby property. Confident that cattle prices would rebound, Tilley trucked his fattened steers to Adelaide, achieving $90 a head in the sales yard. His profit after transport and agistment was $8,000, so he borrowed the remaining $8,000 from the Esanda finance company. To help with the repayments, he gave up smoking: permanently. This was one of the few times Tilley put up capital for a major purchase. In future he always tried to borrow 100 per cent of what he needed, keeping his capital to expand the business in other ways.

Now to find a pilot. Someone told Tilley he would need a bush pilot, as good bush pilots understood all the risks that came with flying in remote areas and knew how to get the utmost out of the least. It would be the eminently practical Geoff 'Brownie' Browne who became integral in defining the culture of a business that neither man yet knew would redefine the history of charter aviation in Australia.

> Geoff "Brownie" Browne became integral in defining the culture of a business that would redefine the history of charter aviation.

Browne had grown up in Queensland. Tilley had heard about him through his experience working for Jock Bremner, who managed pastoralist Bryce Killen's Scott Creek station.

*

Snakes were a regular hazard on the Tilleys' property. Between the two sheds the family lived in, Jenny kept an area with plants, groundcover and hanging baskets. Watering at night was the best time. One evening around 10 pm Jenny was at the task and John was interstate, as was commonly the case now he had committed to aviation. Jenny suddenly saw an enormous brown snake slithering over her hose. Dropping the hose, she dashed inside, woke Scott and yelled 'Get the gun!'

Top: (L-R) Penny, Gwen, Scott, Kate, Jenny & John Tilley in the Pandamus garden;
Below: Geoff Brown (Brownie) & Tilley in Adelaide.

The gun was always loaded with rat shot. Experience had taught the family that a spray of these pellets had a much better chance of hitting snakes. Scott emerged in his pyjamas and boots and dragging the rifle. He tried a couple of shots at the snake but given it was so large, it kept going with a belly full of rat shot. Scott had now run out of shot and the snake remained at large. Jenny was given the choice -leave the snake to roam or get out the 22 shotgun to kill it. The call was made to load the 22 gauge gun. But as Scott was aiming, the snake took off up the corrugated iron wall of the house and over the junction box. Scott began shooting. Bullets punctured the walls of Jenny's bedroom and somehow missed the electricity box. Injured, the snake disappeared up into the roof. Jenny's daughters were still asleep, so she spent a sleepless night waiting for the snake to drop down from the ceiling into the girls' room.

Early next morning, Jenny found the snake outside in the gap next to the family bathroom curled up ready to strike. Thankfully, it was dead.

The 12 gauge bullet holes had passed through three walls in the house, lodging in the walls and ceiling of the nursery, just above the 'meatsafe' cot where baby Penny slept. It had been a lucky escape for Tilley's youngest.

*

Scott Tilley tells a story to illustrate his father's early business acumen. In the mid 1970s when the cattle market was bad, Scott travelled with his dad to Mt Bundy Station, then owned by the large American company W.R. Grace & Co The manager was selling a herd of weaner heifers for around $45 a head and John Tilley always had an eye for a deal, so he bought.

A few weeks later the local Elders manager, Ian Millard, arrived at Pandamus to inspect some cattle John had for sale at $120 each. Scott knew Millard a bit, so felt comfortable adding to the conversation. While Tilley and Ian were leaning against the cattle race as the herd filed past, Scott piped up: 'Whatever happened to those weaners that you bought from Mt Bundy for $45 a head?'

His father glared at his son, then took him out of earshot of his buyer. 'Don't ever talk business again!' he grimaced. 'These are the heifers I'm trying to sell for $120 a head.'

'He was definitely a trader,' Scott admits.

*

In the 1970s the authorities did not require you to have a charter licence if you were flying your own goods. Termed 'aerial work', it suited Tilley. Uralla Meats could start freight immediately, calling the business 'NT Aerial Work'.

Len's fresh Katherine meat sold like hot cakes in Milingimbi and other missions in Northern Australia. Len did not have a mind for profit, loss and business, so Tilley ran the financials, paying the wages each fortnight. Meanwhile, Lennie organised the practical side of staffing, cattle and abattoir operations. Geoff Browne ended up flying in 1,200 kilos each week to meet the needs of just that mission. Elcho Island was the next to take up the offer. A 440-kilo load was all the single engine Cessna's could handle, so each load could only go to one mission community.

In a matter of months John spotted another opportunity: supplying fresh bread to the same missions. The local mission shops already had a deal with a Darwin bakery at 60 cents a loaf, selling it at $1.30. It was only when John queried their freight costs that the mission realised they were paying the equivalent of 90 cents a

Left: (L-R): John, Sarah, Penny, Jenny & Scott Tilley at home circa mid 1976;
Above: Lennie and Patsy Hayes

loaf in freight. They were losing 20 cents on each sale. John worked out he could buy from Katherine's baker for 60 cents a loaf and, adding his costs in, sell to the missions with lower freight costs. The cargo pod of the Cessna, along with the space behind the pilot, could fit around 660 loaves.

At Gove, their meat was coming by steamship from Brisbane. Gove had a Woolworths, a bank and a butcher's shop, so Len's brother bought the local butcher shop and they flew in their fresh rump steaks from Katherine a few times weekly. It was closer, so far more cost effective than a competitor flying meat in from Darwin.

Tilley quickly added weekly deliveries to Roper River, Numbulwar, Groote Eylandt, Wave Hill and Hooker Creek. Often locals from these remote settlements begged for a ride back to Katherine or to be dropped off somewhere en route. Tilley would have been happy for the extra work but his hands were tied: without a government-issued charter licence his plane could not carry paying passengers.

In a short space of time Tilley bought out the Gove butcher business. Its turnover of some $10,000 each week would in time be handy to demonstrate cash flow to his aviation lenders.

*

It was somewhat of a waste for Tilley's aircraft to be returning to Katherine empty. For any successful freight operator backloading, or finding a load for the return leg, maximised your investment, so Tilley decided to import bananas each week from the Arnhem Land Progress Aboriginal Corporation (ALPA), run by the Uniting Church in Nhulunbuy, then sell these into the Katherine supermarkets.

To avoid an empty aircraft on his return flights Tilley decided to import bananas from Arnhem Land.

The bananas were not always a saleable load. If the supermarket had not sold last week's stock they would refuse the next delivery, and Scott Tilley recalls having to dump hundreds of kilos on the family property. The household would be consuming banana milkshakes, banana splits, banana bread and raw bananas for weeks. Until his father invested in a cold store, the stench of rancid bananas would build up on Pandamus' unofficial rubbish dump. Scott Tilley has never since been able to stomach a cooked banana.

*

Often Lennie would buy young cattle in the wet season and fatten them on Pandamus, but there were times when the local supply could not keep pace with demand. The local beasts, Shorthorns, were as Tilley admits 'shit cattle', bred mostly for low-quality hamburger mince for export to the US. 'We ended up having to buy meat from Melbourne as well, cryovacced.'

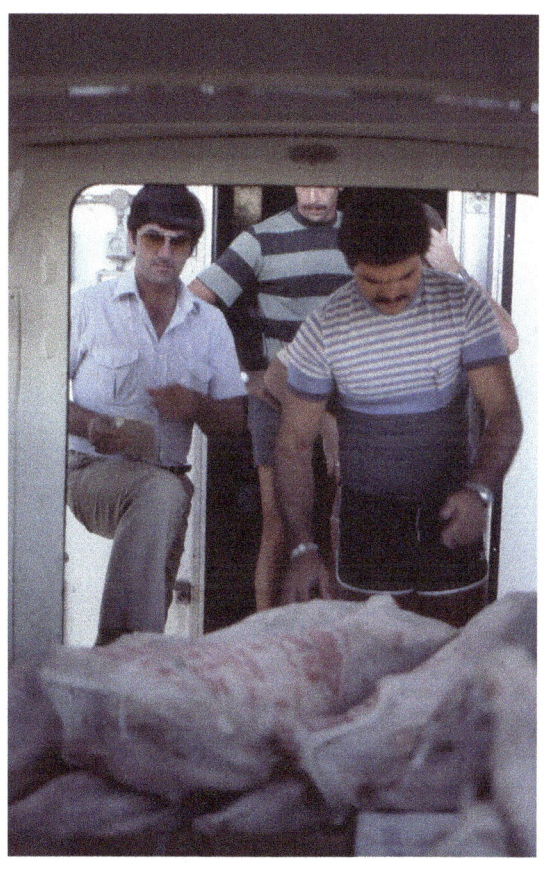

Tilley recalls one Melbourne wholesale company offered him a few tonnes of rump steak at a good price, so Tilley placed the order. The road shipment arrived from Melbourne without labelling on the cartons, and when they opened the cartons they found the distributors had turned the cartons inside out to hide the Vestey's Meatworks in Wyndham brand. Wyndham was just 600 kilometres west. Taking advantage of highly discounted backloading rates, the consignment had travelled by ship 3,500 kilometres south to Perth, been switched to rail and shipped another 3,500 kilometres to Melbourne, then 3,500 kilometres north to Katherine by road.

Poor meat quality in the Territory did not change until the late 1970s, when Brahmans were more commonly bred. Soon enough the Uralla Meats Cessna was delivering to remote communities every day.

Tilley tallies up as pilots load frozen meat bound for remote communities

FIGHTING FOR A CHARTER LICENCE

Tilley still yearned for a charter licence. The only operator with such a licence from Katherine was SAATAS. Headquartered in Adelaide, SAATAS's twin-engine Beechcraft Barons held a monopoly, yet its regional offices were in Darwin and Alice. SAATAS's focus was passenger services and looking after Telecom technicians servicing the remote HF radio telephones on the missions and cattle stations, which were always breaking down. (A condition of the Telecom contract was that a twin-engine aircraft be employed.) The SAATAS Katherine pilot would just sit at home waiting for the phone to ring. Meanwhile, John Tilley was out in the community building connections and loyalty.

The other Territory airline, Connair, founded by aviator Edward 'Eddie' Connellan in 1939, also had one of these much-

The Mighty "Duck" 206 TLU - Much loved.... despite being the slow workhorse of the single engine fleet

DEPARTMENT OF TRANSPORT
S.A./N.T. REGION
68 GRENFELL STREET, ADELAIDE 5000

Box 2270, G.P.O.
Adelaide, S.A. 5001

Telephone: 223 9911
Telegrams: "AVIAT Adelaide"
Telex: 82857

In reply quote 62/1/120

28 OCT 1976

Mr. M.J. Tilley,
Box 710 P.O.,
KATHERINE N.T. 5780

Dear Sir,

I refer to your letter requesting serious consideration being given to granting a charter licence for operations within the Northern Territory, based at Katherine.

As no doubt you are aware, for a considerable time the issue of charter licences in the Northern Territory has been strictly controlled and the Department in its considerations takes into account economic matters. This is a firm policy.

For many years SAATAS has kept an aircraft based at Katherine on a bare break-even basis therefore any erosion of traffic could seriously lessen the viability of the operation to the detriment of the Katherine and surrounding communities. You refer, however, to the untapped potential and I would be pleased to receive your expounded views on this matter.

The Connair dispute has now been resolved and the services reinstated on a modified basis. At the present time it is not proposed to issue any new charter licences but the situation and future developments will be closely watched.

Your application has been given serious consideration but, in view of the factors referred to above, has not been approved. In the event, however, of Connair services being completely withdrawn or drastically reduced and alternative air services are being planned your application will be taken into account.

Yours faithfully,

K.L. COLLETT
for REGIONAL DIRECTOR

coveted licences out of Darwin and Alice Springs. Decades earlier Connellan had negotiated to provide the first mail service between Alice Springs and Wyndham. Eddie had the right political connections, so despite running far larger and more expensive four-engine Heron aircraft, government subsidies meant the business survived. However, Connair was never going to turn a profit so it too started dropping outback stations from once-regular mail deliveries. There was inadequate revenue to justify the work.

Tilley soon had seventeen Territory stations crying out for cost-effective mail and freight services, but SAATAS was not interested in the business. The needs of remote station owners were being ignored. Then in September 1976 Connair was the target of the pilot's union, which was keen to break the stalemate on pilot wage indexation guidelines. With some pilots earning only $6,900 annually, the union decided that by forcing an agreement with Connair, the nation's smallest airline, for a wage rise of 20 per cent for Heron pilots it could use this as a precedent to do the same with the majors.

Connellan had never been good at staff relations, which proved to be a problem when every one of Connair's pilots was convinced to strike. It made front-page news in the Alice Springs paper, *Centralian Advocate*. Many outback stations suddenly had no access to mail or perishable goods. In retaliation, the government withdrew Connair's rights to fly its Herons on its most profitable daily route from Alice Springs to Mount Isa and Cairns, awarding it instead as a once-weekly route to Ansett's jet aircraft.

Due to losing that route, Connair could no longer offer its pilots more than 600 flying hours annually and its flying crew costs per aircraft mile skyrocketed by 50 per cent overnight. Connellan would later claim his operation's losses to be at least $650,000. Given the loss of their major Cairns route, half of Connair's pilots had to be laid off and the company scrambled to find funds for the severance pay owed.

In 1976 Tilley wrote to the federal transport department, applying for licences to allow to carry out aerial service work in not the Territory, Queensland and Western Australia.

Though he had no charter licence John Tilley jumped in to fill the gap, delivering perishables to the Roper River storekeeper among others.

On 7 October 1976 Tilley wrote to the federal transport department, applying for licences to allow his Cessna to carry out aerial service work in not only the Territory, but also in Queensland and Western Australia. He also applied for a coveted charter licence for the Katherine district. If granted it would be a game changer economically, allowing him to take paying passengers. There was huge 'untapped potential', Tilley argued, to deliver services to the outback.

The aerial work licence applications were quickly granted but the department pushed back on a charter licence. SAATAS's Katherine aircraft, the department argued, was running 'on a bare break-even basis', so another licence was not economically viable.

> He also applied for a coveted charter licence for the Katherine district.

However, the department's regional director left the door open for Tilley to explain more about this 'untapped potential'.

Tilley's pressure as well as the trouble Connair was in spurred the government to launch an interdepartmental committee to consult with remote station owners about their mail and air service needs. Northern Territory speaker of the Legislative Assembly John 'Les' MacFarlane, a friend of John Tilley's, also wrote to the federal transport minister Peter Nixon, arguing the case for a second charter licence.

When in January 1977 SAATAS's managing director Bob Burden heard of MacFarlane's intervention to support Tilley he was furious. He wrote to the government from his Adelaide office. Yes, SAATAS's twin-engine service had never been commercially viable from Katherine, but he begged that SAATAS be allowed to offer a single-engine service as well. Tilley's application must be denied.

*

Meanwhile, Connair suffered a further tragic setback. On 4 January 1977 a disgruntled former employee, 23-year-old Colin Forman, drove 2,000 kilometres from Mount Isa to Wyndham, stopping overnight in Katherine. His target was his old boss, Connair's Alice Springs manager, who had fired him months previously.

Forman had worked at the Wyndham aerodrome, so he knew where the fuel key was stored. The next morning, after discovering the larger aircraft he had wanted was out with the Royal Flying Doctor Service that day, he sighted instead a twin-engine Beechcraft Baron. Alice Springs was four hours' flying time, so he filled the fuel tank to capacity. Forman had planned to strike at 10 am during Connair's morning break, but he did not account for the ninety-minute time difference and arrived at 11.00 am.

As he reached Alice Springs Airport, Forman broadcast a final message by radio: 'It is better to die with honour than live without it.' The young pilot then set full power on both engines and lined up his descent to come in between the two aircraft hangars; he knew the Connair offices were on the first floor between the hangars. He plunged the aircraft into the centre of the building, killing himself on impact.

His target was not in the building, but three Connair employees died instantly, including Eddie Connellan's eldest son, 33-year-old Roger, groomed as his successor, as well as two engineers. A secretary was badly injured by burning petrol from the burst fuel tanks and died in hospital five days later. Two more engineers, Tony Byrnes and Kym Hansen, sustained burns to more than half their bodies. It was Australia's first aircraft-assisted suicide attack. With Eddie approaching the age of 65 and fighting cancer, the future of Connair looked awful.

In the years to come Tillair's chief engineer would make regular trips to Alice Springs to service aeroplanes, often working alone until 3 am. At odd times the hangar's huge doors would bang closed, and the bloke swears the ghosts of that tragic suicide mission remained in the building.

> **John Tilley refused to relent in his quest for charter work.**

*

John Tilley refused to relent in his quest for charter work, writing to the Territory's federal member Stephen 'Sam' Calder. Without hesitation, Calder wrote to Minister Nixon to support Tilley's fight to provide regional services. Ted Hart, owner of Hodgson River Station, also wrote to the department, voicing his support, as did Bill Tapp from Killarney Station, who was also president of the Northern Territory's Cattlemen's Association.

With Connair now facing increasing financial difficulties given the federal government had slashed its mail subsidises, you might wonder how Tilley thought he had a chance of making a go of such a business. In March 1977 Tilley handwrote another letter, this time to the awkwardly named 'Inter-departmental committee on Airlinks currently served by Connair':

Dear Sir

Katherine is a very central point in relation to the majority of the Top End. It is closer to the north coast settlements of Oenepelli, Maningrida, Millingimbi (sic), Elcho Island etc than Darwin and of course is much closer to the Roper River and Victoria River districts . . . In most cases goods that find their way into Darwin pass through Katherine & then are flown from Darwin to outlying areas and passing over the top of Katherine. This is particularly the case with perishable & frozen goods. What a waste in time and money? . . .

All goods that are presently flown into Arnhem Land and the pastoral properties in the Roper & VRD [Victoria River Downs] could be offloaded in Katherine & flown out from here, hence saving the cost of haulage by road to Darwin and then air back over Katherine. This at present particularly applies to all perishables . . . It would be easy to organise all perishable items to be dispersed from Katherine. Storage and cool room facilities would be required plus someone here to organise & if granted a charter licence. I would look after this side as well.

The mail and perishable runs I feel need servicing are Tindal, Bullman, Mainoru, Mountain Valley, Roper Bar, Roper Valley, Nutwood Downs, Hodgson River, Hodgson Downs, Moroak, Goondooloo, Tindal, Wave Hill Station, Camfield, Mt Sandford, VRD, Humbert River, Moolooloo, Kidman Springs, Killarney, Delamere-Tindal.

*

With Uralla Meats orders increasing every week and optimistic about getting that charter license, one Cessna was no longer enough. In April 1977 Tilley purchased an additional second-hand Cessna U206F VH-CJG from Rossair. He needed another pilot.

When 19 year-old Gary 'Box' Boxall flew to Katherine the next month for a job interview, he was told that Tilley was the accountant for the local meatworks. Boxall was offered $130 per week in wages, which meant that by the time he paid for his accommodation and meals there would be little left over. The teenager found himself flat out, taking off at daylight and working long days. Some days he might not finish until midnight.

*

By August 1977 it was clear government clients were unhappy with what their SAATAS contract was delivering, and the construction department complained. SAATAS aircraft were late for scheduled take-off times and were unable to provide even one single-engine aircraft. Instead, the department had to pay additional premiums to charter a nine-seater aircraft for just one government staffer.

Meanwhile, in consultation with the Northern Territory Legislative Assembly and the interdepartmental committee, the transport department called for tenders for the Territory's subsidised mail runs. Tilley put in a quote of $20,280 to manage these contracts from Katherine ($137,000 in today's values); SAATAS's quote was nearly 30 per cent higher.

Although he had received a recommendation in May, it was not until 20 October that the Minister for Transport finally approved the issue of new charter licences. Connair's financial troubles had been taking up much of his time. Threatening to close, the government agreed in early October to inject a massive $650,000 subsidy into Connair to keep it afloat.

It was not until October 1977 that the Minister for Transport finally issued charter licences.

The new charter licences went to Chartair in Alice Springs, Tilley in Katherine and Trevor McDonald in Tennant Creek. Just as crucial, there would be financial subsidies to undertake Connair's mail services out of Alice Springs, Tilley's out of Katherine and McDonald's from Tennant Creek. SAATAS was furious. The method of seeking offers was 'unconventional', SAATAS's chairman Richard Cavill complained, 'and could give rise to legal challenge'. The department gained confirmation from its assistant crown solicitor: its approach had been correct.

PARLIAMENT OF AUSTRALIA · THE SENATE

SENATOR B. F. KILGARIFF
6th FLOOR, HOOKER BUILDING,
47 MITCHELL STREET, DARWIN. N.T. 5790
P.O. BOX 4795, DARWIN. N.T. 5794
Phone: 089/813567

25 October, 1977

Mr. John Tilley,
P.O. Box 710,
KATHERINE   NT   5780

Dear John,

A short note to offer my congratulations on being issued your air charter licence. It is most pleasing to see you have been ultimately successful though it has taken many submissions over the last few years.

An air charter licence is a great achievement and I wish you all the very best for the future.

Yours sincerely,

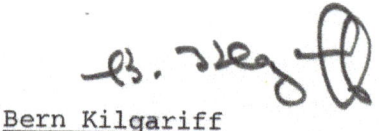

Bern Kilgariff

*

Tillair was at last able to deliver urgently needed mail, perishables and spare parts to the cattle stations and remote Aboriginal communities and receive government subsidies in the process. These subsidies would be critical to giving the fledgling airline its start. Despite the fact that official government approval had not yet come through Tilley chanced it, commencing mail deliveries to all the stations from Katherine that he could. He would bill the government later.

So began Tillair, with a fleet of just two single-engine Cessna 206 planes. Tilley did his calculations: he would need at least three new pilots and more aircraft to maximise the opportunities. Leasing SAATAS's now-redundant Beechcraft Baron, Tillair took over the lucrative Telecom technician work, but he needed a plane that could carry far more cargo and passengers.

The size of the Territory lends itself to aviation. Tilley realised that if he had the courage to invest there was money to be made: someone would always want to go somewhere in a hurry, and in Australia's Top End the lack of accessible roads and huge distances meant a reliance on air transport.

> **Tillair started with a fleet of just two single-engine Cessna 206 planes, but John was ready to purchase his forst new plane.**

In November 1977 Tilley was ready to purchase his first new plane, a Cessna 210 VH-MDZ worth around $70,000. He travelled to Sydney's Cessna dealership, Rex Aviation, where for the first time he came in contact with chief engineer Ron Hoenger. Hoenger recalls Tilley's standard greeting of 'How you doing?' was as laconic as it was distinctive. It would be Hoenger, years later, who would play a crucial role in Tilley's business success.

SEIZING OPPORTUNITIES

Like Connair, SAATAS was financially struggling. Its chairman Richard Cavill rang a senior transport department official to ask what would happen if he closed down. 'There would be a lot of red faces and that's it,' replied the official. 'You are not getting any support at all.'

On 23 March 1978, Cavill sent Peter Nixon a telex saying his directors were considering closing their Northern Territory operations the following week. By the end of March SAATAS was out, and 41 staff were out of work and seventeen redundant aircraft needed buyers. SAATAS's routes from Darwin, Alice Springs, Ayers Rock, Katherine, Maningrida, Gove and Groote Eylandt were suddenly up for grabs.

Cavill released a vicious press statement accusing the minister and the National Country Party of giving Connair 'massive and unfair government assistance': $650,000 *was* a huge subsidy). Cavill said it was pork-barrel politics and discrimination, and he wanted a royal commission to investigate 'financial and government links between air companies in the Territory and the National Country Party'.

In 1979, NT politician Les McFarlane & his wife came to celebrate Tilley's $313,000 purchase of a Cessna Titan 404 TLE. Pilot Brian Wilcox (Snoopy) is at left

Two politicians, he argued, were past Connair directors and the vice president of the National Country Party in Alice Springs was a current Connair director. Not only that, but a past president of the party's Northern Territory executive was a Chartair director. The discrimination was worthy of a high court challenge. Cavill stated that he had been refused meetings with Minister Nixon. 'We can compete against Connair but we cannot compete with the Commonwealth.' Cavill repeated his charges on two national media outlets the next evening, *AM* and *This Day Tonight*.

In parliament on 2 May the transport minister gave a scathing rebuttal of Cavill's accusations. Connair was an established provider of regular passenger services; SAATAS was just a charter operator. 'Charter operators cannot expect to be given a guaranteed monopoly by governments. SAATAS was given an equal opportunity to bid for two routes. In both instances their bid was higher than the successful bidders, Chartair and Tillair.

'The charges question the integrity not only of myself as Minister for Transport, but of officers of my department, the directors of Connair Pty Ltd, of the owners and operators of several charter air services in central Australia.'

> **With the two large charter operators declining, John Tilley saw and seized the opportunity.**

*

It was Tilley who benefited from the ongoing troubles between the established players. With SAATAS, the country's biggest charter operator, now out of the Territory, if he played his cards right John Tilley had the ability to fill the vacuum.

One of Tilley's first government jobs was to do with seasonal fire control. The government needed a plane to help set up backburns to control or prevent bushfires in the dry season around the Hooker Creek and Western Australia border regions. At first the government demanded a twin-engine plane for the work, so Tilley had to lease a Britten-Norman Islander from Transwest in Perth.

To stop a fire that was out of control, recalls Gary Boxall, 'We would fly downwind of the fire front and drop rubber pellets out of the aircraft to start backburns . . . You needed to inject the pellets to prime them then drop them down a chute every 20 seconds, where they would fall a few hundred feet and ignite.'

On one such backburn the departmental worker suddenly started yelling and shoving all the pellets he could down the chute. He had mixed up the primed pellets and tossed some by mistake back into the storage box. It was impossible to tell which had been primed, so he was frantically shoving the entire lot out the narrow chute before they ignited and blew up the plane.

*

Tilley employed four more pilots: Brian Wilcox (everyone called him 'Snoopy') and Peter 'Quinny' Quinn, who both came over from SAATAS now it had lost its Katherine contract. Puffing on his pipe, Snoopy had the demeanour of an older World War Two naval pilot: he was much older than the others and had flown planes in Indonesia. A young Paul Ballard and John 'Marcho' Marchant also won positions.

> **Federal and Territory politicians and government employees were regular passengers on Tillair.**

Les MacFarlane was one of Tillair's first regular passengers, given the government paid for him to travel home to his remote Territory station each week after parliament. Les would fly from Darwin to Katherine on the Ansett service on a Saturday morning, then at 2 o'clock he would provide a government voucher and a Tillair pilot would fly him out to his Moroak station. At 3.00 pm on Sunday a Tillair pilot would fly back out and return the politician to Katherine to meet the Ansett plane to Darwin.

In 1978 the Northern Territory was finally awarded self-government, which meant Grants Commission officials suddenly had a need to visit remote Territory locations to assess applications for state monies. Tillair was kept busy. Pilot Gary Boxall recalls flying a group of Territory representatives out to Roper River to open a new primary school. As he was preparing to descend, he and the politicians noticed a huge amount of smoke. Upon landing, they discovered it was the new school that was burning. The local community had set it alight, angry that their own tribe had not been employed to help build the expensive structure, so there was no school to open that day. For the rebuild the government did at least this time engage the local community to help out.

*

In April 1978 Jenny and John Tilley's fourth child, Kate Maree, was born.

Back at Pandamus on 17 April 1978, Jenny gave birth to Tilley's fourth child, Kate Maree, in the Katherine hospital.

Travelling with John could be tedious, Jenny admits. In every airport they visited John would know someone and was quickly deep in conversation with them. 'John's talent is as a communicator,' Jenny admits. To while away the time Jenny took up reading, ensuring she always had a book to take out on trips with her husband.

There were many times, though, that John set off without Jenny on a trip, and he was never one to share his plans. Most times he'd have his overnight bag with him while going past the front window of the kitchen, and Jenny would confront him. 'I know you've told everyone in the office where you're going [he probably hadn't]. Do you reckon you could tell me? He might say: "I'm going to Adelaide, Sydney and Brisbane," and he'd ring me from Perth.'

Jenny kept herself busy in John's absence; she played squash and had the kids to raise and there was a lot of school stuff, yet she admits she did get 'pissed off' at his constant absences. 'Whatever happened was more important than what I was doing.'

Usually John would leave on a Friday if he had an interstate meeting the next Monday. 'Why do you do that?' Jenny would challenge. 'It means we can't do anything [as a family] on the weekends.' However, work was such a focus for John and Jenny became used to doing things by herself. When John was around Jenny might say: 'We've got such and such on.' If John said, 'Oh, I don't feel like it,' Jenny felt like killing him. Stuck at home for long weeks, Jenny might be devastated.

*

In October 1978 Tilley purchased his first twin-engine plane, a Cessna 310 Tango Whisky Yankee. Without capital in the business Tilley borrowed money entirely on the basis of cash flow, and managing cash flow effectively became the key to his success. By June 1979 Tilley had purchased a 12-seater Cessna 404 VH-TLE, the first of this type to come to Australia.

The toughest thing for John Marchant, who became Tilley's chief pilot when Brian Wilcox retired in October 1979, was keeping up with Tilley's aircraft acquisitions. Marchant needed to deal with the regulators' requirements, which meant operational manuals and delegating pilots to various locations and routes. He frequently felt overloaded.

Tilley opened an office in the Railway Arcade on Katherine Terrace in the old railway building. Something of a rabbit warren, most of the building's windows had bars on them. Tillair occupied the back end of the building. The entry was from the side alleyway, and there was a small reception area then a hallway leading to the kitchen and Tilley's office. The pilots would kick back in the kitchen after a flight to rest and have a cuppa.

> **Over the next decade this fledgling general aviation business saw phenomenal growth.**

Over the next decade this fledgling general aviation business saw phenomenal growth.

*

Left: (L-R): Jenny Tilley with daughters Penny, Kate & Sarah, waiting for dad to return at Katherine's Tindall airport

With self-government came big opportunities for Tilley. Before the Territory achieved self-government federal public servants rarely visited, but that all changed. 'They'd come up for two years in Darwin and Katherine, then go back to Canberra,' Tilley says. 'There was plenty of money coming from Canberra, including . . . Grants Commission contracts to go out and improve the airstrips and housing and schools . . . They'd come up, all these executive government blokes, and we'd fly them around to all these remote places . . . in the big Cessna 404.'

The government executives would inspect the disadvantaged community then fly back to Canberra and approve the proposed spend. 'Everyone was young. The politicians were all young and enthusiastic,' Tilley recalls.

The Territory government was looking at regionalising some of its departments, so it was not just Darwin that housed the Territory's public servants. For Tilley, having taxpayer-funded public servants based in Katherine would be a cash cow, so he lobbied the government to set some departments up in Katherine.

Sure enough, the Territory's departments of transport and works set up in Katherine. It was his relationships with the right people that also quickly secured Tilley all of the region's aero-medical services from Katherine to Tennant Creek and later Gove.

*

By June 1979 Tilley needed a bookkeeper to look after the increasing payroll and accounts with stations, government departments and other customers. Katherine did not have a lot of choice when it came to good office staff, but Tilley struck gold in Milly Goodings.

Milly did not look promising on paper: about to turn 21, she had never done bookkeeping before but Tilley could tell she was smart. Besides which, her husband was Tilley's accountant, Brad. He taught her the basics and she picked it up easily.

Milly recalls: 'I was doing his bookkeeping on written ledger cards and an expenditure analysis book, all handwritten. I used a large calculator with a paper roll attached. Everything was manually calculated and written, including the cashbook reconciliation.'

When the ever growing Tillair operations needed a bookkeeper, young Milly Goodings took charge.

Soon after Milly came on board Tillair won further agreements to deliver mail to remote stations and communities. Previously these had been delivered by truck, so having quicker deliveries by plane was a huge benefit to those areas. It meant Tilley could buy more planes and employ more pilots to handle the workload.

Every six months to a year Tilley would let his bookkeeper know about another growth in the business. Winning the health department's medivac work for the Katherine district was one such arrangement that became very lucrative. With every change, Milly had to ensure that processes were in place to ensure efficient invoicing systems for new clients to maximise cash flow.

As Tilley acquired more planes and more pilots the Katherine office also expanded, occupying more rooms in the building. Milly was moved into a small room with no windows. Feeling closed in, she bought a palm tree in a pot to add some greenery. Apart from an 18-month stint in Darwin, Milly worked for Tilley until November 1986.

TILLAIR: THE INDUSTRY'S EMPLOYER OF CHOICE

In job interviews Tilley was usually adept an assessing whether an aspiring pilot suited his business. He looked for those with ambition, hungry to get their hours and experience up to give them the best chance of a prized career in commercial aviation.

Tillair pilots were often flying on their own many hundreds of miles from assistance. Radio contact with ground authorities was intermittent, depending on how close you were to one of the few air traffic control centres at Darwin or Alice Springs, so the last thing Tilley needed in the remote Territory landscape was pilots who could not think for themselves, take calculated risks and problem solve should they run into hurdles. Tilley's chief pilots, John Marchant or Geoff Browne, would take the young hopefuls up for a test flight, assessing how they coped when presented with an instrument failure or worse.

> *Tilley selected pilots with ambition, hungry to get their hours and experience up, giving them the best chance of a prized career in commercial aviation.*

John Tilley was reviewing 30 applications a week from young pilots keen to secure a job with plenty of flying hours available. Most general aviation airlines wanted pilots with at least 500 to 1,000 flying hours under their belt, such a policy keeping insurance premiums more reasonable. Tilley took a different approach: he was prepared to give young, inexperienced pilots direct from flying school a break 'before they had picked up bad habits'.

Shayne 'Gecko' George reflects about when he joined in 1984: 'There was not another operator in Australia that had a fleet that was that new and provided the opportunity for someone like myself, who had zero experience.' Eager nineteen year olds completing flying school would often write to over 100 general aviation operators around the country looking for work and would be lucky to receive three or four replies. It was Tilley who was often prepared to give these guys an interview.

Over the nine years from 1978, scores of prospective young pilots arrived in Katherine for an interview. Some arrived on Ansett and TAA flights, some drove three days from Australia's east coast, while others took the bus. They all had one dream: to acquire a position with a man who offered the best chance of a future job in commercial aviation.

> **Scores of hopeful young pilots arrived in Katherine for an interview**

In interviews, Tilley always asked what the young trainees' future plans were. If they said they wanted to get into commercial aviation with the big airlines Tilley gave them a tick. He liked ambition. Says later chief engineer Ron Hoenger: 'We wanted guys who had a bit of nous. If they were in a remote location 500 miles from base with no radio contact, flying an aircraft with a minor fault, we wanted guys capable of making a decision to get the aeroplane home.'

*

In the middle of a Sydney winter, Mike Lucas bought himself a one-way ticket to Darwin and started doorknocking all the general aviation companies there. He had packed all his jumpers, having no idea that winter didn't exist in the Territory. In Darwin somebody told him to go to Katherine to meet John Tilley.

For a city kid like Lucas, the vast open spaces of the Territory were an eye-opener. He admits the learning experience was significant: 'Just getting a map and a compass and plotting . . . places on a world aeronautical chart as you went . . . There was always a bit of head scratching. Are you sure that . . . where you think you are is where you actually are?'

*

Mark 'Jerdo' Jerdan, who was labouring on a Sydney building site, put a bet on the Sydney Cup and won $800. 'I've got the petrol money; let's go north,' he announced to his pilot mates. He drove up with Mike Rees north to Mount Isa, then Darwin and Katherine. Tilley interviewed Jerdan and Rees together, confessing he only needed one pilot.

'So, who's got the car?' he asked them.

'It's my car,' Mike Rees replied.

'So, if I give you the job what happens?'

'Well, I'll give Jerdo the car and he can keep driving looking for work.'

Tilley was quick to point out that in Katherine you needed your own vehicle to get around. 'Well, I don't really need two of you, so I won't be able to pay you both normal rate. You'll have to take a lower rate, but I'll take you both on probation.'

*

Gordon 'Gundy' Ramsay went through a book listing 150 Australian charter operators, typing up letters to each one. Only four replied, and none had a position available. A month later Ramsay was just finishing training when Tilley rang: there was a position going but he was interviewing three people. The salary offer was $130 per week, but $45 of that would go on hostel accommodation costs.

'Are you willing to come up?'

To Ramsay, it was the chance to short circuit what might be years of job hunting.

'If you get the job you'll need a khaki uniform: shorts and a short-sleeved shirt.'

Gordon agreed. 'I'll be in the uniform.' He had one day to source the required gear, and in mid-winter in Canberra his chances looked unlikely. Then his mother suggested he try the scout shop.

On the Monday morning Ramsay jumped on the TAA DC-9 from Canberra to Melbourne via Adelaide to Alice Springs. He changed onto the Fokker Friendship flight to Tennant Creek, then Katherine. Picked up by 'Bob the Bastard', appropriately nicknamed because he was the nicest guy, Gordon was dropped at the Commonwealth Hostel in town. The single men's quarters were run by an old dragon called Merl, who was always highly suspicious of the young men. Two bedrooms shared a common bathroom. You could just rent the room or take room and board, which gave you dinner in the dining room.

Arriving around sunset, young pilot Mark Jerdan shoved a beer in Ramsay's hand and cooked Rhim a steak with half a tomato. Ramsay drank slightly too many beers and the next day

Geoff Browne took him up for a test flight, giving him scenarios like engine failure to see how he would react.

Brownie called all the shots when it came to Tillair's operational side, as well as hiring and firing. Tim Travers-Jones, who flew years later for Tillair, became close mates with the man. Travers-Jones had grown up in the bush, flying light planes with his father around Narromine. After flying school at Cessnock he went back to Narromine, but found he was chasing cattle more than he was flying aeroplanes. Flying was his passion, and he heard Tillair was one of the few who offered new graduates a chance. The only other options for those with so few hours was picking up work flying tourists on repetitive scenic flights.

'He was very vigilant and he was very fair and he was very firm,' Tim says of Brownie, 'and he was very well respected. He would kick your butt if you made a mistake . . . He was the bloke that you had to keep on side as a young pilot.' Anyway, Brownie must have been satisfied enough with Gordon Ramsay's test flight, as he scored the job.

Being from Canberra, Ramsay had never seen a stubby cooler, so when a few days later he was handed one he poured his beer in. The other blokes laughed as it dripped out as fast as he could pour.

*

Tim McCubbin arrived from the city reasonably well dressed. It was the tail end of the wet season and the river level was rising. Before he had time to change, Tilley got McCubbin to drive out to Pandamus and pull the pump up out of the river, to save it from sinking. As he dragged the pump up the bank McCubbin sank knee deep into the riverbank mud. When he returned to the office with his city clothes now unrecognisable, 'Most of the boys thought that was pretty bloody hilarious,' McCubbin recalls.

> **Brownie called the shots with Tillairs operations, including hiring and firing. He was responsible to add the young Gordon Ramsay, Tim McCubbin, Barney Milosev and Shayne George to the team of pilots.**

*

Gordon Ramsay's first solo day at Tillair, 25 July 1980 with C206 TL

Barney Milosev was a Perth-based boy from a Yugoslav migrant family. He had been cattle spotting in light aircraft on Palmer Valley station, south of Alice Springs, to get some hours up. The job required you to fly low above the herd and talk to the bull catchers on the ground, directing them to where the cattle were. The step up from this would be mustering cattle by plane, chasing the cows and sending them in a particular direction. It involved flying just above the trees, so was inherently more dangerous. It was a career progression Barney could do without.

He applied to Tillair and in September 1980 caught the DC-9 flight to Port Hedland and on to Darwin. There he had to change to the Northern Airlines Metroliner to Katherine but this last flight was delayed while awaiting a VIP passenger. As he approached, the ground service people said, 'Oh, hello, Mr Tilley. Yes, we're all ready to go for you.'

Barney knew little about Tillair's Katherine operation, so he got to chatting with his potential boss. 'What's involved, what sort of flying? . . . Do you do any cattle mustering?' he asked nervously.

On arrival in Katherine, Tilley gave Barney a lift to the Commonwealth Hostel, introducing the landlady Merl and organising a room. That evening, when all the pilots came back from their flying, they congregated on the balcony drinking beers. Barney crawled out of his room, thinking he had better be social. Mark Jerdan was there, VB in his hand. As Barney approached, Jerdan slapped a VB stubby in his hand. 'G'day, I'm Jerdo. Have one of these.'

Gordon Ramsay recalls Barney driving a fancy rotary engine Mazda around Katherine. Barney's mother would mail him fresh undies and socks each week so he didn't have to do laundry. The other pilots ribbed him and some wagered the guy would be too soft to survive, but they were proven wrong. Barney would become one of Tilley's most legendary pilots.

*

Shayne George recalls getting a phone call from Katherine after sending in an application. 'When can you come up for an interview?'

'I'll be there in three days,' Shayne was quick to reply. He flew to Darwin and then rented a car to drive down to Katherine for the interview. Spotting a public toilet on the median strip in town, he went in and changed into a half decent shirt, a tie and a pair of trousers. After an hour's interview with Tilley, Shayne was told: 'Okay. You start tomorrow. Just don't wear that tie.'

Shayne bought himself an LJ Torana to get about and found an empty unit to rent in Katherine. Tilley had been renting out a battered old caravan to Tillair pilots and Shayne later convinced his boss to buy the unit, which meant Tilley could dock his pilots $60 per week for rent on the three-bedroom place.

> **Tilley knew the oportunities he was offering were in high demand.**

It was 14 months before Shayne George had time to return home.

*

Tilley knew the opportunities he was offering were in high demand. The airline business was very slow right through the 1980s, and

Above: Shayne George (Gecko) and boggy Paul Grant (in blue) loading C210 - TFF in Katherine

commercial airlines were only taking on twenty or so pilots a year. 'We were all glad to have jobs that would put a bit of food on the table,' recalls Ian Lucas.

It meant Tilley could pay his pilots the minimum wage and work them hard: seven days a week. 'He didn't pay us fantastically well. When the term "wage freeze" was being bandied around in Australia, we used to say when it comes to wage freezing John Tilley is an Eskimo,' Ian Lucas jokes. 'Nonetheless, we never, ever waited for money from him.'

A young Mike 'Mick' Cottell spent 30 hours travelling by bus from Brisbane to Katherine for a job interview, only to have the manager say there was nothing available. He spent another 30 hours returning by bus to Brisbane, but a few months later he received a call: 'You want a job? Get up here.' Mick got back on the bus. Being given the opportunity meant 'you went the extra mile to do the best you could'.

*

When Peter 'Junior' Davies started at Tillair in 1985 as a nineteen year old he had come out of flying school at Cessnock with 'basically a taxi licence. Tillair was like a little airline: a one-gig job,' Davies explains. You went from flying a small 'bug smasher' right up to piloting a turbo prop. It was unusual in general aviation for a pilot to have just one general aviation job before graduating to the commercial airlines 'To go to a slightly bigger aeroplane, most guys would have to change companies,' Davies says.

Davies admits Geoff Browne 'was a bit of a hard ass, and he would straighten you out, decide, you know, whether you stay or go . . . If they were going to keep you, then Geoff would decide where you went. The guys who were particularly good went out to the Gulf country and really operated on their own . . . and the rest of us would go to where there would be other pilots around. So you'd get a bit more mentoring and . . . someone would have their eye on you.'

His time at Tillair was excellent training, Davies admits. 'You had to get yourself out of trouble. So you developed a bit of rat cunning and a healthy respect for the risks. One of the things you learn pretty quickly when you come out of flying school: you really over navigate. You want to know exactly where you are . . . so you're identifying little creeks and all sorts of stuff. Whereas the key is just to wait for the big bits, a major road or an escarpment or a big river.

'That's one of the fundamental differences now with the guys coming through into the airline is they're mostly cadets, so they've never really got lost, never really scared themselves.'

One of Davies' first trips was in a group charter to Gove with three Tillair aeroplanes. Out for a beer at the end of the day's flying, the senior pilot Hugh 'Who Coon' Cohen put his arm around Davies' shoulder. 'The way it is up here, there's no seniority,' Cohen counselled him.

But then Davies recalls that once they arrived at the car to return to their digs Cohen commanded: 'Get in the back, Junior.' The third pilot thought Cohen's remark was so funny the nickname stuck.

Above: Tilley's young pilots would be assigned to babysit Kate, Sarah & Penny, known locally as the Tillettes ~ 1981

*

The regulations meant that pilots were only allowed to fly a maximum of six days a week, but whenever his boys were not flying Tilley found alternative work for them: picking up the frozen meat from the cold room at Pandamus and bringing it out to the airstrip; driving the Tillair van around town to pick up freight that needed to be delivered out to stations; offloading the weekly 1,000-kilo load of bananas from the Cessna 404 and hawking the fruit to each of Katherine's three supermarkets.

'You weren't allowed back at the Tillair office 'til all the bananas were gone,' recalls Gordon Ramsay, so you went to the fussiest customer first: Mrs Samalios at Happy Corner supermarket, then it was on to Cox's Store, who were the second fussiest. Finally, you would sell what you could to Katherine Stores. Whatever was left over went back to the office, where Tilley would give you a lecture about not selling all the stock. The remaining boxes would be sent out on the next day's mail run as a gift to Tilley's favourite station owners, or ones he had to pacify after a recent screw up.

Tillair pilots would backload 400 kilos of fresh fish from Maningrida. Kids' clothing (Bema Wear) sown by local women on Bathurst Island was a further commodity that Tilley could mark up and move on to sell in the desert communities on the mainland.

> **New pilot recruits were on probation doing menial obs around Katerine. They were referred to as 'boggies'**

The extracurricular work Tilley assigned his young charges went far beyond banana delivery and sales. New pilot recruits were all on probation, and during this time were referred to as a 'boggy'. For their first few months boggies weren't flying at all; instead, they were kept around Katherine so the team could keep an eye on them. Boggies were given all the menial jobs.

If then fully employed by Tilley a boggy was given his official Tillair nickname by the other, more senior pilots, similar to a fighter pilot's call sign. Some of these are still renowned today: Rowdy, SOMF, Ringers, Muckabin, Dangles, ML, Woodgreen, Marcho, Gundy, Chronic, Junior, Jerdo, Gecko, Who, Possum, Lurch. Only one, Andrew Maclean, though rising to great heights as a Tillair pilot was forever known as 'Boggie'.

Boggies found themselves picking all the stones out of the tracks in the hangar doors so the doors would slide smoothly. The trick was to always be busy, which could mean making sure the office bins were never full and always looking for something to do. Tilley owned Katherine's Budget Car Rental franchise, so there were always cars for the boggies to wash and occasionally new ones to drive down from Darwin. Then there were babysitting duties for the 'Tillettes': Tilley's three daughters.

There was seldom a complaint, because in exchange the Tillair boys were rewarded in other ways. Most general aviation airlines ran older, clapped-out aircraft but not Tilley, who always ensured he leased or purchased the newest Cessnas available. Mike Lucas recalls that the Tillair planes were very smart compared to it some of the older, worn-out aircraft competitors flew around the Territory.

THINKING FOR THEMSELVES

After ground-based duties, the next step up would be a mail run in one of the smallest planes. The very first flight assigned to young Tim McCubbin in March 1980 was the bread delivery to Maningrida on the Arnhem Land coast. It was the tail end of the wet season, which meant thunderstorms were a daily occurrence, and as a new pilot McCubbin had never flown in this sort of weather. Fifty boxes needed to be loaded in the Cessna 206 but only 47 boxes would fit, so the remaining loaves needed to be unpacked from their boxes and squeezed into the aircraft's remaining nooks and crannies.

'You can't get lost,' Brownie assured him. 'If you hit the sea, you know you're close.'

McCubbin was about halfway to Maningrida when he looked out at a massive wall of water in front of him. He swore loudly. 'Oh, my god. This is way out of my league.' He turned around and radioed ahead to explain the appalling weather was way beyond his experience.

When he landed back in Katherine one of the older pilots, George Westmacott, was on hand with a Cessna 310. 'Give us a hand,' Brownie grunted. 'Throw the bread into the 310 and George

Left top: Tim McCubbin in 402 TZH; Centre: This 402 TZH, with Mike Lucas (M-L) and young engineer Colin Barge illustrates the limited storage space and access for freight. Bottom: Pilot Peter Davies refuelling at a remote station on the south-west mail run out of Katherine

will take it up there. He's got plenty of experience flying in that sort of weather.'

McCubbin was rueful. He had managed just half a flight with Tillair and now he was sure Tilley was going to sack him. 'It wouldn't have been unusual for some of the other operators to do just that.' McCubbin admits. In fact, McCubbin's decision to turn back confirmed in Tilley's mind that he was worth keeping. It meant McCubbin knew his limitations and was not going to 'bend one of my aeroplanes trying to do something he couldn't do'. However, at the time Tilley said nothing. Only decades later did he explain his thinking to McCubbin.

Says McCubbin, 'He's a very good reader of people and personalities, which is why it was not unusual for blokes to be given their marching orders within two or three weeks of starting at Katherine, because John would realise that they weren't going to fit in.'

*

Barney Milosev's first flight on his own was the regular run in the Cessna 206 VH-TLU to Milingimbi to deliver bread and perishables: potatoes, fruit and meat. It was the dry season and controlled burns were everywhere, which meant the visibility was awful. As a new pilot Barney was only licensed for visual flying, which meant relying on maps and visual landmarks. Barney did find Milingimbi and offloaded the goods.

Coming back towards Katherine and flying at 10,000 feet, he struggled to see the ground for the smoke. The 'Duck' had instruments to give you a compass reading but was the only plane in the Tillair fleet that lacked any instrument to measure distance. Barney had no idea how far he was from Tindal Airport. All he had to help calculate his location was time and his estimated average speed of two miles a minute. The wild card was the effect of wind speed and information on wind speed for a 206 pilot came only from the weather forecasters, who could be notoriously inaccurate. As he continued flying south, Barney's mental calculations meant there could be a 50-mile error margin in his actual position.

To be unsure of your position in the Territory is fairly common, particularly in bad weather, but you knew roughly where you were and how to get yourself out of it. However, the regulator had a rule stipulating that if a pilot could not specifically state where they were then flight services could take operational control of the aircraft. 'They might ask you to make an immediate turn and head back towards the highway, following it back to Katherine or wherever,' explains Ron Hoenger.

When Barney estimated by his watch he was about 30 miles north of Tindal, he began his descent. Still up at 6,000 feet, Tindal was suddenly below him. 'Oh, god, I've got to get down now,' Barney realised. He put the flap out to get more drag, pulled the throttle back and spiralled down towards the airport below. He landed safely and shut the aeroplane down, only to see John Tilley standing there.

'We were almost like his kids,' Barney recalls. 'His brand-new pilot went on his first flight and he was there to make sure that I got back okay.'

*

When it came to running an airline, says Milly Goodings, Tilley's purchase decisions were based on what was required for the business. 'He would buy a plane because it was the right vehicle for the job,' says Peter Quinn, rather than pilots who ran small airlines, who tended to purchase based on what they would like to fly. Tilley was also gifted in being able to minimise spend in his growing aviation operation.

> **Tilley's aircraft purchase decisions were based on what was required for the business unlike others who would purchase on what they would like to fly.**

His Cessna 206 had fixed wheels that could not be retracted, while the 210 model had a different wing shape and the wheels retracted after takeoff, meaning they could fly 40 knots faster. Some careful calculations showed Tilley that for the same fuel burn costs per hour the Cessna 210 could travel 30 per cent faster than the 206. For the regular mail runs with so many stops en route in one day extra speed was crucial, so Tilley ultimately invested in sixteen of these. Flagged for use on the mail runs, the six seats would be removed and the plane crammed with whatever freight and mail the stations had ordered: bread, fruit, vegetables and tractor and Toyota parts. This was the first route a new Tillair pilot would be tasked with.

*

In the wet season and without radar, pilots were always 'scud running' under the clouds, relying on their local knowledge and counting the rivers. You had to be good at visual navigation, but the Tillair pilots did so much flying that they learned how to re-orient themselves if they got lost.

> **Without radar, pilots were 'scud running' under the clouds, relying on their local knowledge and counting the rivers.**

Pilots had to make regular scheduled calls to let flight services know where they were, and flight services expected to hear from pilots at a certain time. If they received no radio contact ten minutes after expected they would assume the worst. On landing a pilot needed to radio in again so flight services could cancel the SAR alert: the search and rescue watch.

If the strip looked too wet when the pilots flew over, Tilley warned them not to land. Instead, they would do a later run in the Cessna 206 Tango Lima Uniform, nicknamed the 'Duck' given it had non-retractable super-fat tires. It was slower to get around, but it could land anywhere.

Tilley recalls one incidence where a single-engine Cessna piloted by Barney Milosev got bogged in the wet season at Tanumbirini station, the third stop from Katherine on the south-eastern mail run. 'We left him there for three days because we couldn't land,' Tilley admits. 'Brownie ended up landing on the bitumen-sealed Barkly Highway' to go rescue him.

Pilot Keith Tym is a profuse sweater, and with no air-conditioning in the light planes the sweat would pour off him every time he landed. He could tell how many landings he'd done by how far the sweat marks came up the pocket on his shirt.

Rostered to fly the 13-stop western mail run, when he reached his eighth stop at Bullo River Tim Travers-Jones used to spend an extra ten minutes with Sara and Charles Henderson and their three daughters Marlee, Bonnie and Danielle. To save them coming to the airstrip to collect the mail, Tim says, 'They'd leave the gate open from the airstrip and they'd expect you to taxi up to the house and park the Cessna by the pool.' As a trade off they would invite you in for a cool drink, but with so many stops ten minutes was all a pilot could afford if he was to get back to Katherine before dark.

*

As well as the newest aircraft, Tilley gave his pilots the maximum number of flying hours allowed each year. While officially pilots were not permitted to fly more than 900 hours per year, the work demands were such that many Tillair pilots flew well over this quota – not that their log books showed this. Mark Jerdan reckons there were many hours he never logged. 'The work was there and I was happy to do it . . . It wasn't as if you could call on someone else.'

While they were not being paid extra for the long hours, Tillair pilots were racking up invaluable experience in some of the toughest flying conditions imaginable, and doing this in a time before GPS or satellite navigation was available. They all learned fast.

> **As well as the newest aircraft, Tilley gave his pilots the maximum number of flying hours allowed each year.**

Pilots needed to lodge a flight plan with flight services to report their planned route, how much fuel they were carrying and the number of passengers. Because there was no way to transmit paper documentation, the pilot would ring up reverse charge from Tillair's Katherine office or from the airport out at Tindal. 'They'd be all waiting for a turn to come in and use my phone,' Hoenger recalls. If they were based out at a mission such as Numbulwar with no telephones, the only way to lodge the plan was via radio. Flight services would then give the pilot a weather report.

Because the flight service people monitored pilots' names, pilots figured that the Department of Civil Aviation logged each individual pilot. One pilot explained: 'If you wrote seven days in a row and you had an accident, the aeroplane is not insured, so you won't see anyone that's got seven days straight in their logbook.' Thus, occasionally a Tillair pilot who had overreached his hours for the month would radio in his flight plan using an alias.

*

Keeping the exterior of the Tillair planes clean was a hallmark of the small operation. New pilots were instructed that after a day's flying they needed to spend as much time as necessary with a can of Mr Sheen and a cloth cleaning the entire aircraft fuselage. After a day of landing and taking off from a dozen rough airstrips removing all the oil and dirt could take time, but to a Tillair pilot a clean plane was a badge of honour.

Accruing their hours quickly allowed the younger pilots to be eligible to get their instrument ratings and hence move on to flying Tillair's bigger twin-engine planes. For young pilots, one of Tillair's main attractions was Tilley's strict policy of ensuring pilots achieved the hours needed to progress. Tilley says: 'It wasn't in writing our seniority list . . . but everybody knew where their position was . . . and there was no contract. It was all on done on a handshake.'

> **Everybody knew where their position was. . . and there was no contract. It was all on done on a handshake.**

'It was a great morale booster . . . because you knew when you got your hours up you were going to see some progression,' says Gordon Ramsay. 'You had to have flown 1,000 hours in a single engine before Tilley would put you in a twin engine.'

At this point a young pilot would train to achieve his instrument rating to allow him to fly the twin engines. Once they had this and their senior commercial licence, Tillair pilots were allowed to carry passengers at night. Once a Tillair pilot had clocked upwards of 500 hours in a non-turbo charged twin engine, this milestone allowed graduation to flying a Cessna 402 or 404 Titan, the turbo-charged multi-engine piston.

*

Tim Travers-Jones was a later Tillair recruit. Without sending any letters, not to mention the offer of an interview, in June 1986 the twenty year old drove to Katherine to plead his case. Tim recalls walking into the Tillair office thinking he was smartly dressed: RM Williams boots, jeans with a plaited belt and a blue and white check shirt. A young lady at the front desk snapped back at him, 'Oh, no, we're not hiring. There's nothing, nothing going.'

'I've driven, you know, a long way from New South Wales,' Tim persisted. 'Isn't there a chief pilot I can speak to?'

'No, no, he's out flying . . . There's no one [who] can help you.'

'Oh, well, what about Mr Tilley: any chance I can talk to him?'

'No, no, he doesn't talk to young guys that are pestering him.'

But Tim was not leaving. Finally, the front desk girl agreed to ask. 'But I don't think he'll talk to you,' she warned.

Tilley emerged, wearing exactly the same outfit as the wannabe boggy. He grinned, and said: 'Well, you better come in and have a chat.' The interview must have gone okay, because Tilley agreed. 'We'll see if we can offer you a job.'

If Tim could entertain himself for a few days, Tilley's head pilot would be back and could take him for a test flight.

*

Stuart Palframan still recalls arriving in Katherine in 1986 dressed up in a tie and long trousers for his job interview. A grizzled Geoff Browne turned up in his khaki shirt and runners without socks to take him for a test flight. Palframan felt way over-dressed. Brownie quizzed the youngster on his practical knowledge, and Ron Hoenger took him aside to grill him about the mechanics of planes. Palframan had never flown a Cessna 210, and the experience with these old hands made him realise just how little he knew about aeroplanes.

*

Reflects Ian Lucas: 'Tilley was passionate about his business, and these guys were passionate about aviation. They all wanted to get into the airlines. They all needed to get 3,000 plus flying hours in the best aeroplanes they could, so they worked hard and benefited John. These guys got the flying hours they needed and very quickly moved into the airlines and their future was secure.'

The commercial airlines commonly rang the Tillair office to let a pilot know their application had progressed and to ask if they could come to Sydney for an interview. 'By the time you got back from the mail run,' Barney Milosev recalls, 'the secretary would have organised a flight for you through Ansett.' Tilley would always check if his young charges needed accommodation for their airline pilot interview. 'Do you know someone there that you can stay with?'

'Even if he couldn't spare you,' Barney recalls, '[Tilley] would cross hire another pilot from another company to cover your flying while you were away.'

'Most of us wanted to be pilots from when we were teenagers,' recalls Mike Cottell.

Cottell had a Qantas interview coming up in mid-1988. The day prior, he was booked to do a charter near Borroloola but failed to locate his charter passengers before sunset. By the time he had tracked them down he was forced to overnight in Borroloola, but the next day he was due to catch the Ansett Fokker 28 flight from Katherine to Alice then on to Sydney for his Qantas interview. Cottell calculated that by the time he got into Katherine the Ansett flight would have departed. He was going to miss the interview of his life.

However, out at Tindal Tilley was all over the issue. Cottell's boss had gone to the flight deck and asked Ansett to hold the plane until Cottell boarded. 'So Tilley was directly responsible for getting me to that interview, which shaped the course of my career for the next three decades. I'll never forget him for that,' Cottell reflects. The young pilot was just 23 years old when Qantas took him on.

'The relationship we had with Tilley was almost symbiotic,' Mike Cottell explains. 'He got an enthusiastic, reliable, loyal bunch of guys and in exchange we would go the extra mile because he gave us a chance to get our hours up . . . a career trajectory to get into the airlines and therefore fulfil a dream. We were so grateful . . . He was a catalyst to allow us to have the careers we've had.'

While his competitors would not have stomached it, Tilley was proud whenever one of 'his boys' secured an airline job, so he was forever employing young pilots who would stay just eighteen to 36 months before moving on to the commercial airlines. It meant having to perpetually rehire and retrain but Tilley shared in his young charges' excitement, happy to see them moving up.

> **"We've got to make Tilley money" was the key logic that the senior pilots used. The tricks some pilots used to improve profitability were impressive.**

*

Peter Quinn recalls Tilley 'drove us pretty hard, long hours. The work didn't conform to modern-day union rules or aviation regulatory rules. It was about getting the work done. There was no clocking off at a certain time. [Instead,] we embraced Tilley's survival.'

John 'JT' Torr concurs with Peter Quinn: 'We've got to make Tilley money was the key logic that the senior pilots used. Otherwise the company goes under and you don't have a job.'

The tricks some pilots used to improve profitability were impressive. John Torr again: 'You could take an unpressurised plane to 10,000 feet by law, but . . . there was no radar, so sometimes I went a bit higher. At 11,500 feet you could get a really good tailwind so as to save Tilley some money on fuel.' Torr shrugs. 'You were still 500 feet below a plane authorised to fly at 12,000 feet.'

Standing around the bar in Katherine on a Friday night, Tillair pilots would swap tips. Flying higher than normal in an unpressurised Cessna had another advantage if you had rowdy passengers who were always drunk. The higher altitude meant the oxygen thins out, and it would put them to sleep. 'The pilots who complained, "Oh, we've got to have a rest period here" or "I don't think the runway's right" or "I don't know how to do this,"' John Torr admits, 'they were the ones we weeded out.'

Quinn recalls: 'You would finish work tired, [then] go to the pub and every night have a mixed grill. [This] would turn into a drinking session with the other pilots there, ending in late nights. Driving back to the single men's hostel with too many beers under our belt was common. Early morning [starts] in those days we could carry a hangover. You might be up at 4.30 or 5.00 am in the morning to pick up 660 loaves of bread from the town bakery. While there, I'd scoff a fresh Cornish pasty and a carton of Farmers Union iced coffee for breakfast, then it was on to pick up the meat then help load the plane.'

One pilot recalls there was a strict eight-hour abstinence rule from 'bottle to throttle', though it was not perfect. 'As a young guy you could drink way too many beers and turn up eight hours later feeling fine, but with a lot of alcohol still in your system.' There was no breath testing: 'You just judged it from how you felt.'

> **There was a strict eight-hour abstinence rule from 'bottle to throttle', though it was not perfect.**

GROOTE EYLANDT AND NUMBULWAR

Tilley's operation quickly required basing a pilot and aircraft not just in Katherine but in very remote communities. Groote Eylandt and Numbulwar were the first of these. Basing a plane on these missions meant they could ferry in and out the local Indigenous people, along with health-care workers and occasionally mining staff. Tilley might give a pilot just a few days' notice that they were being seconded to one of these, and sometimes it was for three months and sometimes a year. In Tilley's mind, having a girlfriend or wife made such moves complicated so he wanted his pilots to be single.

Some who Tilley gave a chance to left of their own accord, unprepared to do time in these remote postings. Tilley accepted one lad from a pretty well-to-do family, but when he learned he would be posted to Groote Eylandt or Numbulwar he pulled the pin. The youngster's father flew up to Katherine on a Learjet to bring him back to Sydney.

Groote Eylandt is the largest island in the Gulf of Carpentaria, named by Abel Tasman in 1644. The original inhabitants, the

> *Tilley's operation quickly required basing a pilot and aircraft in very remote communities, such as Groote Eylandt and Numbulwar.*

Anindilyakwa, include fourteen clans proud of their traditions who maintain strong ties with their neighbours in Numbulwar and Bickerton Island. The mining company Groote Eylandt Mining Company (GEMCO), a subsidiary of BHP, had established the township of Alyangula, complete with a pub and golf course, in 1963 for its manganese mine workers. The island's airstrip sat next to Angurugu, one of the island's two key Indigenous communities.

In November 1978, with Groote Eylandt Air Charter's owner in financial trouble, copping 25 per cent interest on his aircraft loans, Tilley bought out his business. Tilley admits the guy he bought the business from did not understand how to structure an aviation loan.

With the sale came a six-seater Beechcraft Bonanza VH-ILG. Tillair pilots concede that compared to Cessnas, Beechcrafts are better built: the door handles never fall off and the trim is nicer, but pilots soon discovered that unlike Cessnas they easily go out of balance with a heavy load. As well, Cessnas are cheaper to buy and the parts are cheaper. If the Cessna trim falls off, you can just glue it back on.

Whenever Tillair's Beechcraft broke down, the dealer would never have the parts required. Tilley recalls Mark Jerdan was taxiing in the Beechcraft when the plane fell into a ditch and something on the nose broke. When Tilley rang to order a replacement part, the Beechcraft technician warned him there would be a 90-day wait. Such delays cost money. 'I'd put the phone down [to the Beechcraft dealer] and the next thing I'd do is ring up and buy another Cessna,' Tilley admits. It was not long before Tilley traded in the Baron and sold off the Bonanza.

By way of comparison, Tilley was so well connected with the supply chain for Cessna parts that when there was a major mishap, his aircraft downtime was minimal. Tilley recalls John Marchant was in a Cessna Conquest doing a medical run. Taxiing to the end of the runway at Waterloo Station, the pilot went beyond the boundary marker to ensure he had plenty of room to get airborne. Suddenly the Cessna fell into a bog hole, damaging both the nose and engine.

'I remember being in Darwin on my phone and rang Garrett in America.' Tilley knew instantly to order a new engine, at a cost of $90,000. 'It was here within two days.' His engineer flew out to the site. 'We jacked it up and put chaff bags underneath and dragged it out of the bog with a Toyota . . . removed the old engine, put in the new one . . . and flew it home. It took a week or two.'

*

For many Tillair pilots, especially in the later years, Groote Eylandt became the outstation of choice. As the island had a major mining site, there were underground aircraft fuel tanks so Tillair pilots could buy fuel locally. If a business client wanted to book a charter flight from Groote they had to ring Tillair in Katherine. The Tillair office would then relay a telex booking to the pilot's lodgings in Groote for him to pick up.

If a local wanted to book a charter flight on the local Aboriginal trusts account they went to Tony. Tony Wurramarrba

Doing a u-turn on a soft airstrip, the wheel of Conquest C441 TFG sunk into the soil such that the propellor hit the ground and bent the blades

was the president of the trust, the big dog among the Aboriginal communities. 'Tony was quite a character,' Tim Travers-Jones recalls. 'He was an old school Aboriginal guy. He never wore a shirt and he had a cross cut on his chest: two big long strings of flesh tied in a knot.'

Locals would go to Tony to get approval and this approval number would be passed on to the Tillair pilot, who would write a docket and bill the trust. Hugh Cohen recalls the locals would knock on the door any time from 6.30 am until sunset to ask for a flight there and then. The common request was to be taken the twenty-minute hop over the water to Numbulwar. Thursdays in the Groote Eylandt community was card night, and Cohen recalls for the $240 charter cost to Numbulwar the locals would count out 48 grubby $5 notes. Often there were a lot more people on board than seats, with each adult nursing a child on their lap. 'We were that bloody happy to be in airplanes that never stopped flying that we never thought of docking cash from Tilley,' says Hugh Cohen.

Each May and June was 'clam time', when millions of dollars in royalties were paid out to the locals. Cohen recalls dozens of distant relatives would turn up from remote parts such as Mornington Island, Darwin and even Queensland. At this time of year it was not unusual for Cohen to be booked to fly a local Darwin person to buy a new car. 'The cash economy was unbelievable.'

*

First thing in the morning on Groote, Barney Milosev recalls, 'I'd jump on our motorbike . . . and most of the time the damn thing wouldn't start . . . So I'd have to fix it before I could go to work and then go out to the airport.' Pilots would wait at the airport for work. A local might come out and ask to be flown to Numbulwar or Gove. If it was quiet, Milosev would jump on the motorbike and drive around the Aboriginal community to see if anybody else wanted to go flying.

For the socially active Mark Jerdan, Groote Eylandt was purgatory. Being alone was hard, given the only times you came into Katherine were for 100-hour scheduled maintenance checks. Tim McCubbin also found his time on Groote Eylandt lonely. He slept in the house of one of the island bosses, taking his meals in the miner's mess or the club down the road. At night he studied for a subject he needed for his senior commercial licence, otherwise he was flying nine or ten hours a day.

Given all payments were in cash, McCubbin was taking $2,500 or more in cash to the bank each week. If there had been a funeral off the island, the takings might be closer to $12,000. 'The ANZ bank people used to hate me because everything was paid in cash, and invariably that would be in $1, $2 and $5 notes or $10 notes. I'd walk into the ANZ bank on Thursday afternoon with shirt pockets and trouser pockets full of scungy bloody $1, $2 and $5

Left: Brad Rogers (Chronic) with 210 FOC on Groote Eylandt. Above Tim Travers-Jones & Ted Landy on the company bike, Groote Eylandt airfield, 1986

notes, hundreds of them, and hand them over the counter and say "Here, count these."

'One day I had a young girl came out to the aeroplane. She wanted to go to Numbulwar and [asked] could I wait there for 20 minutes and bring her back. It was $132 each way, and so I flew her over there and I said, "Look, I'm actually pretty busy, so if you're not back here in 20 minutes I'll have to go and pick you up later."

'I was about to leave and the next thing this motorbike comes flying around the corner and this girl is on the back of it. She jumps in the aeroplane. She's just got a brown paper bag in her hand. All the way over I'm thinking, What the bloody hell is in this brown paper bag? I asked her when she got off, "What's in the bag?"'

'Oh, bag of flour,' and it was a half kilo bag of flour.

'What, you paid 264 bucks to fly over to Numbulwar to buy a half kilo bag of flour?'

'Yeah. Shop closed early in July, and I want to bake a cake.'

'The money had no value to them,' Tim explains. 'It was just a means to do things. It didn't matter whether it's $130 or $50 or $10. If they needed to do something, they handed it over.'

*

The Aboriginal community on Groote was dry. Given the elders would not tolerate their men drunk, hungover or bringing alcohol into the community, if the locals went into the Alyangula mining town club and drank too much then they couldn't go home. They would crash on the side of the road or down the beach before sobering up. Some might be banned for months for getting too drunk and obnoxious, so those who wanted a serious session had to charter the Tillair plane to go somewhere else such as Borroloola. Tim McCubbin flew one notorious Groote Eylandt guy down to Borroloola on a Saturday morning to play cards.

'Can you pick me up on Monday?'

'Yep, but if I get here on Monday and you're drunk or hungover ... I'm going to leave you here and you'd have to get in touch with your wife and I'll come back Tuesday.' Tim returned on Monday but his passenger was still drunk. He flew back on Tuesday: still drunk. Wednesday, the same. Not until Thursday did he turn up sober.

*

Barney Milosev made the mistake once of giving credit to a Groote Eylandt local who pleaded to him: 'My wife's in hospital in Gove. I haven't got the money now [but] I'll get my cheque on Thursday. Can you take me over there?'

Barney says, 'We used to give an hour free waiting time because after that if you were sitting on the ground and not flying, you had to charge . . . about $30 an hour or something.' This time, Barney waited four hours at the Gove airstrip before the guy arrived back, carrying cartons of beer. 'Oh,' Barney said, 'I thought you were going to see your wife in hospital?'

'Yeah, I went there 15 minutes.'

Back in Groote, Barney waited for his money, but every time they guy spotted Barney he'd take off and go the other way. Two weeks later Barney needed to send the takings to Tilley, so he marched up to the elders. 'Okay, the aeroplane's grounded until he pays up.'

'Well, you can't do that.'

'Yes, I can.'

'Well, no, we'll have you sent off the island.'

'Do what you have to do, but I'm not flying till he pays me.'

An hour later the elder was back with the money, having threatened Barney's passenger: 'You pay that pilot, otherwise we gonna kill you.'

*

In 1979 Tilley spent $313,000 on a brand-new twelve-seater Cessna Titan 404 VH-TLE, borrowing the entire amount. It could carry

> **In 1979 Tilley purchased a brand-new Cessna Titan 404 VH-TLE**

ten passengers or 1,200 kilos of freight. Rather than sending a single-engine aircraft to a community twice a week, this aircraft could take a week's supply in one load and thus slash the accrued pilot time and fuel costs. The backload potential for goods such as bananas was also far higher.

By 1979 East-West Airlines sniffed an opportunity in the Territory and wanted to launch a subsidiary, Northern Airlines. The trouble was Tilley had already claimed rights to the Northern Airlines name, so East-West needed to negotiate a deal. Tilley saw an opportunity for himself: he would give up the Northern Airlines name, but in exchange East-West were to share their operational and technical expertise to allow Tilley to streamline his own operations.

Connair remained handicapped by its lack of capital and the death of Roger Connellan. Back in September 1979 Connair's general manager was reporting that engineer and pilot award negotiations had forced annual cost increases of over $215,000, on top of forecast annual losses of over $280,000. Connair's passenger fares were proving poor competition up against Tillair, whose services were expanding like a rocket.

Roger's younger brother Chris had no interest in taking over, so in March 1980 Eddie Connellan signed a deal to sell to East-West's Northern Airlines. East-West retired all Connair's slow and expensive four-engine Heron aircraft, replacing them with Metro turbo-props. The old Connair pilots used to handling the Heron's in and out on gravel airstrips were retained; however, flying a Metro was far more testing. Plagued by bureaucracy as well as the mismatch of pilots to aircraft, the marriage of ex-Connair pilots with Metros failed.

Northern Airlines continued to struggle. By the end of 1980 East-West decided to liquidate its Northern Territory subsidiary, though it was not until mid January 1981 that East-West informed its Territory directors of the closure. With Northern Airlines in receivership, the NT government was furious. However, for Tilley it was pure opportunity: Tillair quickly picked up the Northern Airlines regular passenger routes from Katherine to Roper River and Groote Eylandt.

> **With Northern Airlines in receivership, Tillair quickly picked up their regular passenger routes from Katherine to Roper River and Groote Eylandt.**

Numbulwar is a small Aboriginal community on the Gulf of Carpentaria. Permanent settlement began in 1952 with the founding of the Rose River Mission. Closely tied to the Anindilyakwa culture, which originated in Groote Eylandt, the community maintains its kinship traditions. Many Numbulwar residents had relatives on Groote and locals benefited hugely from the mining royalties paid each quarter to their community.

Left Top: Tilley, David Prior (Daisey) and Ian Menzies with 402 ARJ at Numbulwar
Below: In 1979, NT politician Les McFarlane & his wife came to celebrate Tilley's $313,000 purchase of a Cessna Titan 404 TLE. Pilot Brian Wilcox (Snoopy) is at left

Mission Aviation Fellowship had provided air services for the community until 1981, when a Darwin pilot started taking too many liberties with the local women. The Elders insisted the pilot leave, and the friction meant John Tilley was able to step in with an alternative service.

The size of the settlement varied depending on the seasons, shifting from 400 to 1,000 people. The power supply was intermittent, and there was no television and no telephone. To make a call you had to book it on the HF radio. The operator would say, 'Oh, that'll be in five hours' time,' so five hours later you'd go back and the call would be put through.

With no road access for most of the year and a terrible road for the few months it was passable, 44-gallon drums of aircraft fuel

needed to be shipped in by barge from Darwin and food supplies ordered three months in advance. These also came in by barge from Darwin.

Keith Tym was the first Tillair pilot rostered to Numbular. 'In case you hadn't noticed, I liked to hire country boys,' Tilley told Tym. 'I thought they were a better bet than boys from the city.' Tym recalls his boss sitting him down before he shifted to Numbulwar. 'It's important you do this properly, because the Elders there are very influential. It's one of the few dry communities and they are strong on this, so you can't drink. Do that at Groote or Gove, where it's allowed. You can't even look at the local girls, and cash-only payments before you take off.'

Tym soon learned the Elders had another rule: never fly in a community member if he was still drunk from an off-mission drinking session. Tym was to leave them so the locals could sleep it off and find some money from a friend or relative for a later flight. Early on in his placement Tym misjudged one of his passengers when they turned up for the return flight. 'They looked okay so I took them. They fell asleep on the plane, but back in Numbulwar they caused so much havoc I was brought in front of the Elders and told off.'

> **Keith Tym soon learned the Elders of Numbular had a rule: never fly in a community member if he was still drunk**

*

Gordon Ramsay was the second Tillair pilot at Numbulwar, this time for a six-month stint. He would collect on average $6,000 each week in payments for ferrying the Indigenous locals around, often just 20 minutes across the shark- and crocodile-infested water to Groote Eylandt. Once Tillair started running a regular public transport service that stopped at Numbulwar, the pilots would hand over their bag of cash takings to the more senior Katherine-based pilot to take with him back to head office.

During his time there, Ramsay recalls an unusual incident. A Numbulwar man had murdered a Ngukurr woman, and the Ngukurr community insisted on payback by spearing the culprit. The police vetoed the idea, ruling that the culprit go in front of a Darwin magistrate, but the locals held firm and a compromise was arranged. As long as the victim was not killed and had immediate access to medical care, the police authorities agreed the spearing could go ahead. Once the action had been completed, a waiting LandCruiser would drive the speared man to a plane on standby and medivac him with a doctor to Darwin, then when he had recovered he would face the Darwin magistrate.

An appointed day was set. The communities were only 150 kilometres apart, but the landscape in between was so criss-crossed by near-impassable rivers that the road was only open three months a year. When it was open it was a four-hour drive. Instead, the Numbulwar locals booked Ramsay to ferry four planeloads of their warriors and spears to Ngukurr to take part.

As Ramsay sat in the police LandCruiser at the top of rise watching the old Ngukurr airstrip below, the warriors on each side prepared their face paint before performing a corroboree as a lead-in to the spearing. Finally, the offender was handed over and a large wooden spear thrust into his thigh. Gordon only had time to ferry one planeload home before darkness descended; the last three groups would need to wait until the morning. Such events were a huge win for Tillair revenue.

*

During Mike 'Dangles' Strong's nine months at Numbulwar he inherited a couple of mud-crab pots from the local plumber, who had decided to move interstate. 'They have very large and powerful claws,' Strong recalls. 'If you get your finger inside that claw they will do a lot of damage. They would easily crush a bone.'

Without a boat, Strong just threw the crab pots in off the riverbank. After mastering the art of using the pots and safely handling the catch, he became an occasional supplier of mud crabs to Tillair staff. At the time Peter 'Rowdy' Cook was based across the water on Groote Eylandt. Rowdy tasked his mate with filling a large Esky to surprise his family in Wudinna in South Australia during his upcoming annual leave.

Over the following weeks Mike Strong duly caught and froze in the community shop freezer the required crabs to fill Rowdy's Esky. During a rare Katherine layover, Strong deposited the Esky of frozen crabs in John Tilley's walk-in freezer on his Pandamus property for Rowdy to collect. Sometime later Rowdy headed out to Pandamus to retrieve his Esky for the flight south to Adelaide, but on arrival he was horrified to discover the entire stash had gone missing. It turned out that Tilley had stumbled across the delicacy and, duly applying the possession being nine-tenths of the law principle, he had cooked up and eaten the lot.

A MAINTENANCE DIVISION

After every 100 flying hours, regulation required that aircraft underwent a maintenance check. With no certified maintenance engineers in Katherine, Tilley needed to send his aircraft to Darwin. Peter Quinn recalls that when there was urgent work required, Tilley did call in itinerant local engineer Roy Rayner. 'He did some occasional plane maintenance.'

Rayner lived out of town, so it was easier to fly the aircraft to him rather than risk him driving into Katherine. 'He was a good engineer, helicopter engineer and fixed wing, and he kept us afloat,' recalls Tilley. Years later, Peter Quinn recalls he was killed in a road accident.

By mid-1980 Ansett's Northern Airlines was struggling to make any money on its regular passenger transit (RPT) services that flew twice weekly Darwin–Groote Eylandt return (Tuesday, Thursday) and twice weekly Darwin–Hooker Creek return (Wednesday, Friday). Each was a four-stop run into some of the same remote communities Tilley was running mail runs.

Left: It would be Tilley's chief engineer Ron Hoenger (Ronbo), pictured here in C-210 MDT, who would become the mechanical lynchpin of the fast growing airline

John Tilley was only too happy to pick up the work, and his 12-seater Cessna 404 would be the ideal aircraft for the job. However, this would be Tillair's first RPT ticketed flight. To complicate matters, Ansett and TAA retained the right to provide the Darwin–Katherine leg of each route, which often meant passengers needed two tickets instead of one. Tilley had to work fast to cobble together a booking agent's manual and ticketing system.

Tillair formally took on the routes from 4 August 1980. Tilley engaged consultant Stephen Marshall, who had a background with Connair, to write a 66-page manual. Cobbled together and roneoed within four weeks, the manual spelt out every task for agents in the most basic of language, ensuring they understood how to read a 24-hour clock and contact reservations (still handled by Northern Airlines in Darwin) and where to send their sales returns and ticket copies (Tillair's Katherine office).

The only means of contact with reservations and sales was a landline, telegram, mail or what was labelled 'interport mail': sending stuff with the pilot. Darwin reservations also had a telex machine. Agents had to learn how to fill in ticket coupons and which of the five carbon copies (blue, green, yellow, pink and white) was given to the pilot, head office or the passenger. There were rules around luggage allowances per passenger (16 kg for adults) and what to do if a flight was overbooked (children could share a seat if their joint weight was under 77 kg).

By late that year Tilley was tiring of having to send his planes to Darwin or Alice Springs to be serviced. For every 100-hour Darwin service, Tillair pilots had to overnight at the grotty Leprechaun Motel – nicknamed the 'leprosy lodge' – at Darwin Airport. Tillair needed an engineer in Katherine. Ron Hoenger, regarded as the best Cessna engineer in the country, would be ideal.

> **Tillair needed an engineer in Katherine. Ron Hoenger, regarded as the best Cessna engineer in the country, would be ideal.**

It was good timing: Hoenger was by then experiencing constant staff problems at Rex, along with embarrassing stuff-ups with his team's repairs. He felt let down, and when a Rex Aviation serviced plane nearly crashed Ron had had a gutful. He needed out. He confided in Tilley, who suggested he come and work for him in Katherine.

Hoenger, then 33 years old, was tempted. While running things solo in Katherine it would be only himself to blame. Besides, he'd always had an interest in the outback. Neither he nor wife Ros had ever set foot in the Territory; nonetheless, Hoenger was aware many bush aviation operations could be pretty rough and ready and he was dubious; however, in February 1981 when nineteen-year-old pilot Gordon Ramsay turned up in a uniform in Darwin to fly them south, Hoenger was impressed.

Hoenger took up some parts and did some repairs while he was there. He soon realised that Tillair was a safe, well-managed operation. Chief pilot John Marchant had a background in mechanics so had been doing occasional repairs, but a full-time engineer would be a godsend. The Tindal airbase even had an impressive 3,000-metre runway.

Katherine pleasantly surprised Ron and his wife. With children aged six and nine, it offered a new adventure. To hedge their bets, the Hoengers invested in an enormous caravan to drive up to Katherine. If it did not work out, they could move on. For the first few weeks Tilley hosted them all on his Pandamus block, until they relocated to a Katherine caravan park.

In Katherine, Tilley and Ron Hoenger set up an informal partnership. Tilley established a separate Tillair maintenance division, employing apprentices under Ron to service not only the Tillair planes but those belonging to station owners, the Tennant Creek meatworks plane and mustering aircraft. As well as his Tillair work, Hoenger was paid 30 per cent of all the external maintenance work. Attracting decent engineering apprentices to Katherine was a significant hurdle. In time, Hoenger trained up a few talented locals.

Hoenger respected Tilley's commitment to well-maintained aircraft: it was a business expense he never skimped on. If a plane needed a part Tilley would always tell Hoenger, 'Get the part as quick as you can. It'll be paid off by tomorrow's [charter] job.'

> **Tilley and Ron Hoenger set up an informal partnership with a Tillair maintenance division, employing apprentices under Ron to also service planes belonging to station owners, the Tennant Creek meatworks and mustering aircraft.**

'The first few years were exciting . . . I was flying aeroplanes, I was fixing aeroplanes, going out to remote places. It was all a whole new world to me.' Hoenger admits. 'It was one of the greatest adventures and a really pivotal part of my life. It made me feel like I was someone really worthwhile. Maintenance of aeroplanes is not . . . a menu. [Back then] we were . . . known by our capability. A good engineer was a guy who could make good judgement, knew that if an aeroplane had a problem it could still fly . . . and not be unsafe or [be able to say] "It's unsafe. We don't fly it."

'I was more than just an employee. I considered John more than just a boss. I always considered myself to be working with John.' In fact Hoenger was not an employee, but contracted his services to Tilley.

In time Ron was doing a lot of travel. One week he would be tasked with changing an engine in Birdsville, then the next week an engine would need replacing in Milingimbi. Ron once left home in Katherine, caught a jet to Adelaide and then on to Melbourne to fix one of the fleets jets at Tullamarine. Returning to Alice Springs by noon, he discovered another aircraft needed fixing. By two pm, with that job done, Ron was flying himself back to Katherine when a call came about a plane crippled over the Gove peninsula. It

Left: (Top) Alan Chatfield (Chatty) ready to fly 402C TFD. (Bottom) Four TILLAIR 210s including TFC, RQD & TFI. Tilley never bothered to standardise the paint colours when he purchased a new plane.

meant diverting first to Darwin to collect a new propeller and then south-east to Arnhem Land. Arriving at midnight, the repair took 90 minutes and he flew out again at 2 am, reaching home through a few tropical thunderstorms at 4 am.

The Commonwealth Department of Aviation had rules about who was qualified to sign off on aircraft repairs. An engineer could be certified in five categories: engines, airframes, electrical, instrument and radio repairs. Hoenger had the first two, but such licences were not easy to obtain and remote airports had no other certified engineers. It meant that for aircraft maintained in Katherine or Alice Springs, an appropriate certifier often had to be flown in from Darwin or Adelaide.

In between scheduled maintenance visits, if a repair was needed such as a simple lightbulb change or alternator failure it was easy to fix but it was not practical to fly in a certifier, although this was technically required. In the eyes of the regulator, a failure to have repairs certified was a crime. To get around this ruling, many bush operators including Tillair would do the necessary repairs but simply not document them. Occasionally the Department of Civil Aviation (DCA) would make 'Gestapo raids' on Katherine to check Tillair's maintenance and repair records. Unfailingly, they would seize on a problem with a missing signature, launching further enquiries.

Gordon Ramsay recalls a Tillair aircraft he was flying from Adelaide to Alice Springs on a cargo run. The plane developed a slow oil leak out of Adelaide and the only accredited maintenance site for oil leaks in Garrett engines was in Wagga, so Ramsay radioed chief engineer Ron Hoenger. Rather than abort the flight, Hoenger stayed up all night, guiding the young Ramsay by radio to remote airstrips along the route where he could land every half hour, top up the oil and take off again. Ramsay recalls being directed to tiny airstrips at Leigh Creek, Oodnadatta and others before making it to Alice.

'DCA staff were ex airline engineers,' explains John Torr. 'If they heard about a fault, then there was lots of paperwork. Their engineer has to come out, fit the new engine, certify the work. They didn't understand . . . an outback airstrip.' Instead, 'If you could get away with it, just shut up and do it' was the Tillair motto.

*

In the early 1980s telex machines were what Tilley relied on for contact with the Sydney and US markets, and this was not only in relation to aviation suppliers. Betting on overseas futures markets became something of a hobby for Tilley. While he had a Sydney broker who could keep him abreast of market developments, the telex machine he had installed in the Katherine office would provide a feed of US prices for not only silver and gold, but even pork bellies.

> **Tilley was interested in innovation and efficient reporting and Tillair was the first business in Katherine to take advantage of computer technology..**

'I remember one night silver went up to $120 an ounce, then later there was a rumour that Ronald Reagan had been shot. Well, the bloody silver market collapsed. I was in Tennant Creek . . . at a public phone across the road from the motel, putting in bloody coins, talking to [my broker].' Tilley admits the hobby might one week 'make him a few grand and then you lose a bit . It was a lot of fun. It kept me alert on how the world works in finance.'

Tilley was interested in innovation and efficient reporting. Around 1981 his accountant Brad Goodings (Milly's then husband) convinced him to invest $30,000 in a computer-based

Ron Hoenger's maintenance hangar at Tindall airport, Katherine

aviation system. Revolutionary, it would give the business the ability to track revenue, tickets, manifests, profit and loss. It was an enormous investment for such an operation and a major administrative change, but Tillair would be the first business in Katherine to take advantage of computer technology.

A consultant company TABS was introduced and Milly Goodings worked to build Tillair's own software, with the contractor writing all the necessary code. Milly's windowless office became the air-conditioned computer room. The computer was huge, the size of a large fridge, and the back-up disk was also massive, a big circular cartridge with a handle to lift it in and out of the compartment. With it came an enormous printer, about half the size of the computer, spitting out paper onto a roller with spokes on each side to keep the paper in place. It meant Tilley was able to print out a profit and loss management report on demand for the regulator or his financial lenders. They even sold the software to other small airlines such as SkyWest in Western Australia.

Tilley recalls: 'All the data was in a big round thing at the bottom of the computer, and supposedly we had to take it out at night and take it home in case the office burned down.'

In the years to come, as Tillair expanded, opening branches around the country, updated computers were purchased. Each time the computers would get smaller and more powerful. Katherine attracted a great deal of electrical storms in the wet season, risking power failures, so the last Tillair computer system cost $250,000 given it came with a battery back-up system.

Milly moved into Tilley's original office and was allowed to pick a new desk, made of solid American oak. 'I loved it and I loved my job.' By 1981 Milly was effectively Tilley's accounts and administration manager yet, perhaps given his male-focused upbringing, Tilley never referred to her as anything but his bookkeeper. To Milly's frustration, Tilley's dyslexia meant he never spelt her name correctly. He always wrote 'Millie'.

*

Tilley recalls one incident 700 miles north-west of Alice Springs. The bosses of Shell had flown up in their private jet from Essendon, Melbourne to Alice Springs to go out to inspect an oil-drilling site. The Tillair pilot took them out and found the landing strip, but there was no windsock. As he was coming in to land the pilot realised the wind was coming from the wrong direction. Aborting the landing, he circled back and approached from the other direction. However, he forget to lower the wheels and they belly-flopped onto the sand strip. Another Tillair pilot had to fly out and pick them up. Meanwhile, the company engineers needed to jack the stranded plane up and make repairs to the propeller.

'I don't know how they got it up on its wheels again. I didn't ask,' Tilley admits.

His engineers flew the plane 700 kilometres back to Alice Springs but there was no maintenance capacity to make the repairs there for 18 months, so Tilley asked the aviation department for permission to fly the plane on to Sydney to have the repairs done there. They refused. 'They're a pain in the arse, fuckin' government. We flew it for 700 bloody miles with new props . . . but they wouldn't let us fly to Sydney.'

THE TILLAIR TABLET

TO BE TAKEN ONCE A MONTH!

ISSUE No.2   SEPT 82   COST 50¢   WEATHER Very Hot   Page 1

ROWDY REPRIEVE FROM TROPICAL PARADISE!

AAP-TART,KATHERINE MONDAY GROOTE EYLANDT declared a day of mourning when Pilot Mr.Rowdy Cook was returned from his command,trouble is they have not decided on the day as it was only yesterday when he was discovered missing. When Mr.Rowdy was asked to comment on how he felt about the move he said "nonetoo soon" when asked to expand on his comment s his reply was swift " UUHH !".Rowdy has been replaced by Ex boggy Ringers who was last seen walking into Town after his Bike chain allegedly broke.Mr.Rowdy pictured right is seen to be having a quite drink at home after a hard day's flying. Mr.Rowdy was again interviewed and gave us some very rare insights into the life style of the distant Pilot,everything from smuggling to mountaineering with Leg's long time associate Ralph. Ralph declined the opertunity to be interviewed as she was off to climb Lovers Leap the HARD way.Rowdy leaves us for 6 weeks holiday.

DINGOES LIE LOW AS DUCKS BUZ OVERHEAD

TAS-YYP RAILWAY TERRACE FRIDAY Dingoes have gone to ground at the appearance of low flying Ducks (Terminology for a type of aircraft a C206 with fat-wheel s)on the horizon,for they know only to well it is the dingo Terminators LEGS & LUCAS what a dangerous combination. Never before have such a concentration of Ducks appeared in the Northern Territory skys except for that most dreaded of all things-except being based at abbit Flat-Dingo Baiting.As we go to press reports have been received that the Dingoes were banding together to protest for land rights,legal opinion is also being sought.Spokesthing for the Dingoes said that if the Aboriginal s can make a claim then he could not see how they could disregard their faithful & only true friends.The Ducks can be easily recognised-by the swam of blow flies that follow them in Company.When asked about his task' Jucas one of the leading Dingo hunters in Australia just gave a wave of his two fingers,our raving reporter took this to mean that he was ready to go out for yet another adventure.We can only wish them both well as they fly of into that great unknown world of the Dingo....

FACTS ??
* COMMITTEE - A group of people who individually can do nothing, but collectively can meet and decide that nothing can be done.

** STILL REQUIRE CONTRIBUTIONS **

GOVE

By 1982 Tilley had proven his pilots' and aircrafts' worth, and the Northern Territory aeromedical service agreed to use his planes for the remote Gove and Arnhem Land communities. Tilley negotiated hard so that his aircraft also had the right to take paid charter work out of Gove, as long as they gave medevac work priority. Their first medevac work was done with the Cessna 206 with the balloon tyres, the Duck, simply because it could get into landing strips that the bigger Darwin- or Alice-based twin-engine planes could not.

> **In 1982 the Northern Territory aeromedical service agreed to use his planes for the remote Gove and Arnhem Land communities.**

Mike Lucas recalls in the wet season it could be hard to tell if an airstrip was going to be too boggy to land on. Sometimes you could radio ahead to the station owner, and they would 'get in their old Toyotas and run up and down the airstrip and see whether they left a track or not'. Then they would radio the pilot to let him know.

In time, Tillair also convinced the government to let its teams do the medevac work out of Katherine, as well as ferrying local nurses to conduct their regular clinics in remote communities. In the past young nurses had spent days driving in government Toyotas to these remote missions and days driving back to Katherine.

By 1982, Tilley's staff were penning a satirical newsletter to entertain each other

Young Gordon Ramsay was dispatched to Gove for the next twelve months. These days such an arrangement would require three pilots working shifts at triple the cost, but Tilley in typical fashion said: 'One pilot, one plane, that'll do. If you want to go drinking, ring up the doctor to see if anything's happening.' For Ramsay, this involved much judicious management of his beer intake. Because few strips had any landing lights, once the sun set it was unlikely he would be needed until the next morning unless the medical situation was critical or the tiny Gove hospital needed a medevac to Darwin, so he would check to see if any medical situations were deteriorating or there were pending emergencies before going to the pub.

*

Tim McCubbin recalls run-ins with Tilley were not common, but one in particular stood out for him. He was based in Gove at the time and bringing the aeroplane in to Katherine for a 100-hour maintenance check. McCubbin was really looking forward to a weekend back at base with some of the other pilots, but a call for a charter had just come in head office to pick up some Indigenous men in Borroloola and fly them down to Mornington Island at the bottom of the Gulf for a big Aboriginal ceremony. Minutes after he arrived in Katherine, Tilley told McCubbin to get back in another plane. 'You're going to Mornington Island for the weekend.'

Tim was pissed off. 'It's a pretty long way to Mornington Island. I've just flown down from Gove. What accommodation have you organised for me?'

'You'll find something when you get down there.' Tilley blew him off.

McCubbin did a quick calculation: if he left straight away he could land at Mornington Island by 5.00 pm, which would give him time to drop his passengers and fly back to Robinson River station before dark, where he knew the owners would welcome him for a social weekend. However, it was nearly dark when he landed at Mornington Island and that meant there was no option but to stay on the island. McCubbin came across some maintenance workers repairing the airstrip. 'Anywhere I can stay tonight?'

'Oh, just come and stay with us.' They were camping in a local hall. 'You can throw a swag on the floor there.'

McCubbin settled in. He was soon to learn that the ceremonial weekend marked the first in six weeks that grog had been allowed on the island. The allocation was two cans of beer per person, but when the quota was drunk the locals wanted more. A sizeable number raided the store as the local police attempted to stop them.

'It got completely out of hand,' McCubbin recalls. He and the maintenance workers decided to lay low inside the hall. 'As the night went on, it became pretty apparent that the shit was hitting the fan outside. A couple of the local men thought that we probably had some grog, so they decided that they'd bash their way into the hall.'

McCubbin locked the doors and they armed themselves with anything available. 'The next thing we knew they'd poured petrol around the outside. What the fuck? They're going to set fire to this. We're going to get bloody burned alive.'

McCubbin and the other blokes looked at each other. Outside, the police station was being trashed, then the rioters next attempted to break into the health centre. It was a nasty situation, and the police radioed for reinforcements from Cairns. Somehow, the hall was not set alight and in the early morning hours the town finally fell silent. McCubbin got a few hours of fitful sleep, but the next morning he was still in a state of shock.

I'm not hanging around here, McCubbin decided. He passed the word around: he was taking off at 10.00. If his passengers were not there he was leaving them behind. They all piled in and he booted them out at Borroloola, returning alone to Katherine. By the time he arrived at Tindal his passengers had been on the phone to Tilley to complain. 'The bloody pilot wouldn't let us stay . . . for the Sunday part of the ceremony.'

Tilley went berserk at McCubbin. 'But you can't do this to Aborigines. You can't do this to our good customers!'

'Are you going to hear my side of the story?' McCubbin was furious and stormed off.

On the Monday morning McCubbin picked up a pile of Australian newspapers off the freight flight from Adelaide. The

front page was taken up by the story of a Mornington Island riot. A policemen had been seriously injured and the police station and a number of other buildings badly damaged by fire. McCubbin grabbed a paper and stormed into the Katherine office.

'Is Tilley here?' he asked Jan Cole, Tilley's secretary.

'He's on the phone to the chief minister.'

'Tough.' McCubbin barged in, slamming the newspaper down on Tilley's desk. 'Read that,' he grunted, before turning around and walking out to the little room where the pilots used to gather.

After reading the piece, Tilley came over. 'Oh, it sounds like you had a good weekend at Mornington Island.'

'Yeah, well, would've been nice if you'd heard my side of the story. You're lucky to still have a serviceable aircraft and pilot.' McCubbin reflects, 'That was probably the worst interaction I had with John. He didn't apologise. That wasn't his way, but at least he understood what had happened. To be honest . . . that was a period when the business was growing at a phenomenal rate. John was trying to run it on his own . . . He was under a fair bit of stress . . . trying to keep up with the expansion.'

Indeed, by then the little airline was providing mail runs and ticketed services to more than 100 towns and communities in the

Territory and Western Australia and South Australia. On any day in the Territory there might be 21 Tillair planes in the air.

*

When Shayne George was flying for Tillair in the Territory, he recalls most of the accommodation didn't have any air-conditioning. Instead, they had ceiling fans and floor-to-ceiling louvres that you opened. To cope with the humidity, Shayne would lie in bed and use a bottle to spray water above him with the ceiling fan going. The water would almost evaporate before it came back down.

Mark Jerdan recalls just how tough the tropical heat could be in Katherine. 'We didn't want to put on our shirts in the morning. In preparing the planes, given the 38 degree heat and 100 per cent humidity, your clothes would be dripping wet before you welcomed your first passenger.' Jerdo would take off his shorts and shirt, hang them on the wing and prepare the plane in his undies.

> **Tilley was never a believer in leasing aircraft. For larger aircraft he might enter a deal to lease but always with the option to purchase a few years on.**

Another pilot arrived at the Katherine base to find the seats not re-installed after the freight run the day before. To save himself working up a sweat, he decided to throw the seats in and fix them once in the air. When the plane was at 8,000 feet the temperature was far cooler, so he switched to autopilot and left the cockpit to install them properly down the back.

*

Tilley was never a believer in leasing aircraft. For larger aircraft he might enter a deal to lease but always with the option to purchase a few years on. For loans of $500,000 upwards, it was American and Japanese lenders such as Rothschild and Capital Finance whom he tended to work with. Tilley would get a profit/loss report printed out on the office's dot matrix printer and sent in the airmail bag to his Sydney finance brokers. In later years Tilley would develop his own relationships with these banks, making a broker redundant.

Left: Gordon Ramsay (Gundy) with Tilley's new million dollar 441 II Conquest KDN in early 1982

*

By 1981 Tilley had around seven aircraft. He had purchased the Gove butcher's shop from Lennie Haye's brother and was servicing the locals and works at the large bauxite mine. It meant there was enough demand to use the Cessna 404 every Monday to freight fresh meat to Gove, bringing Gove bananas back to Katherine as the backload.

One of the reasons for Tilley's success was his ability to match the ideal aircraft to the tasks at hand. Soon he calculated that it would be better to upgrade his Cessna 404s to pressurised Cessna Conquest turbo-props, given these offered more efficiency: their turbine engines meant they had more capacity and burned less fuel. The plane's price tag was close to $1 million, but by then there was sufficient cash flow in the business to keep his lenders happy.

> *One of the reasons for Tilley's success was his ability to match the ideal aircraft to the tasks at hand.*

In late 1981 Tilley sold his Cessna 404s and invested in a Cessna Conquest. To be eligible to fly these prop-jet aircraft his pilots needed to have at least 3,000 hours under their belts, but by then Tilley had several with that level of experience. He sent John Marchant to Sydney to become endorsed on his new purchase and bring the aircraft back to Katherine. The switch was also timely in regard to medevac work for the government: if a patient had heart trouble or certain other medical conditions a pressurised cabin was necessary, so the Conquest ticked that box.

Tilley had an unwritten agreement with Airnorth's John Hardy in Darwin that Airnorth would limit its operations to north of Pine Creek and Tilley would service the communities south of a horizontal line going through that town.

John Tilley soon bought out Trevor McDonald's Tennant Air, a small operation that came with two planes but, more importantly, valuable subsidised mail runs. From Tennant Creek the 2,500 square kilometre Ucharonidge Station was the first stop on Barney Milosev's once-weekly mail run. The station owners, Mick Beebe and his family, were really nice people, Barney recalls. 'They knew us young pilots were probably out late the night before . . . [so] they would ask "Have you had breakfast yet?"'

'Actually, I haven't.'

'Okay. Go and see the cook, he'll make you bacon and eggs.'

The hospitality gave the station owners time to open the mail bag and read and reply to any urgent letters on the spot before Barney had scraped his plate clean.

The interior of Tillair's first Conquest TFG could be fitted out for executive travel.

LIFE AND DEATH

A key agreement Tilley arranged from the early 1980s was for the air ambulance work out of Katherine, which required their team to have a pilot on hand 24/7 for patient retrieval. The Katherine hospital might get a call from Hooker Creek to say: 'We have a girl down here in labour.' Government policy by then was to offer such cases a taxpayer-funded emergency airlift to the nearest hospital. A Tillair pilot would need to land, pick up the patient and fly her to Katherine to ensure a medically supported birth.

Shayne George recalls one medevac call-out at 2.00 am for an alleged king brown snake bite requiring pick-up from a remote community strip. The locals would place a Toyota at either end of the airstrip in the grass and stand on the brakes to give the approaching pilot a couple of red lights to mark the end of the runway. Shayne also needed someone to light the left and right sides of the runway, so he called the local contact on the radio. Kerosene bowl lanterns with a wick was the standard offer.

'Have you got that strip lit up for me?'

An Aboriginal voice crackled back, 'Yeah, we got him lit up . . . one side of him lit up.'

'Which side?'

'The left side.'

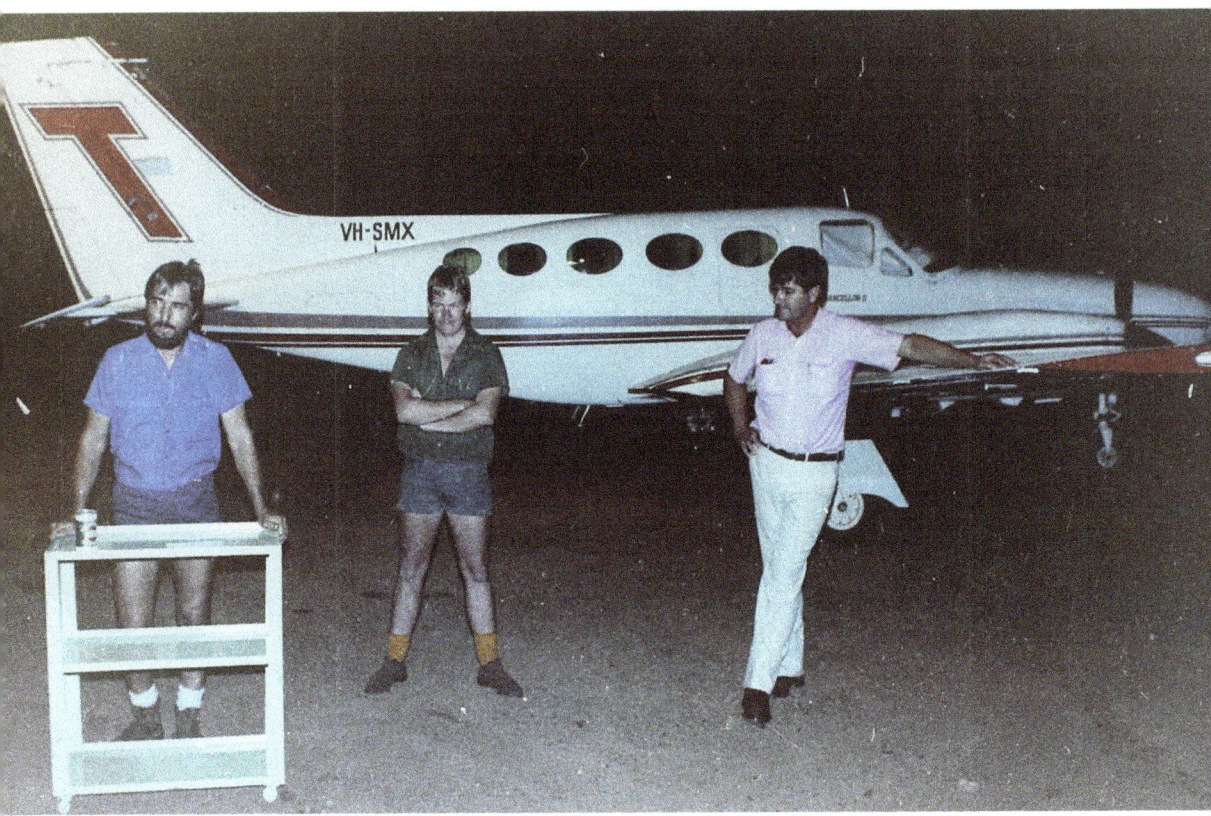

'Go out there and light both sides. I don't know if it's your left or my left.'

When Shayne arrived, his Aboriginal patient greeted him. 'Hey, Jane!' He couldn't pronounce 'Shayne'. 'Do you think I could sit up the front?'

'What do you reckon?' Shayne scowled. 'You get in the back.' Once back at Katherine base, the bite turned out to be a double wasp sting.

The government compensated Tillair $1,500 for each of these medevac cases, then there was additional revenue from the ticket the same patient purchased some days later to take them home.

*

Jokingly, John Torr explains: 'In Katherine, whichever pilot was on call for medevac duties was assigned a pager by the hospital. When we were all drinking down at the pub, whoever had the can of light beer when the pager went: he had to take it'. In fact, being placed on pager duties meant an early night so as to be ready for anything, plus the possibility of a few more hours in the logbook.

On 22 March 1984, a 23-year-old John Torr flew out a Katherine medevac nurse, Gloria Duffy, to run a clinic at Hooker Creek. On the way back Torr received a radio message: 'Can you divert to Victoria River Downs? There's a lady, Olga Bobby, in trouble, having trouble with a birth.'

Torr recalls, 'We strapped a stretcher onto two seats and strapped her onto the stretcher.'

Once airborne, Gloria warned Torr: 'I might need your help. I think she's going to give birth.'

There was no way young Torr was going near a newborn. Instead, he froze at the controls, pretending the autopilot was broken. 'Sorry, I'm going to have to stay here.' The next thing he knew, a baby girl was crying. Once in reach of Katherine air traffic control, Torr radioed in to amend the 'passengers on board': 'We've now got six passengers, not five.'

The next day the story was a feature in the local paper.

*

During Tim McCubbin's Gove posting in 1982 he received a call-out for a pregnant mum in trouble in Milingimbi. He raced over from Gove with a nurse to find they had just missed the birth. The baby was healthy enough but the mum was in serious distress, and even before McCubbin had her on the stretcher she was dead.

They left the body on the aeroplane stretcher and flew her into Gove. McCubbin radioed ahead to organise an ambulance; however, a corpse was not a priority call and both Gove's ambulances were busy. With the body still in the plane, McCubbin needed help offloading it. He estimated she weighed at least 90 kilos. Another Tillair pilot, Grant Colman, 'built like a brick dunny and not afraid of anything', McCubbin recalls, happened to come in and land, so McCubbin walked over.

Ron Hoenger; Col Barge; Tilley with the pressurised 414A SMX.

'Grant, mate, I need you to come and give me a hand. I've got a body in the back of the aeroplane and we need to get it out because I've got a fair idea that I'm about to get called out to go somewhere else. We'll just put it in a cool part of the hangar.'

'Fuck off! No, I'm not getting in there. She's dead. I'm not getting in the bloody aeroplane with a dead person.' Grant would not go near the plane.

*

Two weeks later the Cessna 402 had gone to Katherine for its 100-hour maintenance check. A smaller Cessna 310 was the temporary replacement to take health-care staff out to community clinics, but for the emergency that unravelled that week the smaller plane would prove challenging.

It was late afternoon on Friday, 25 June when McCubbin received a phone call: an urgent evacuation to Darwin was needed for a woman having serious birth complications. At about 7.00 pm Tim met the two nurses, the doctor and pregnant patient at Gove Airport. It would be a two-hour flight to Darwin

'When the baby's born on the aeroplane . . .' the doctor began, giving instructions.

'Bullshit, mate: a bloody baby's not gonna be born on my plane,' McCubbin protested. 'Why the hell aren't you doing the birth in Gove hospital?' he continued.

'Off you go.' The doctor was adamant.

McCubbin's mind flashed back to the Milingimbi new mum who had not made it just two weeks earlier. 'It's a fairly small six-seat Cessna 310 with just enough room to lie a stretcher behind the right-hand pilot seat. The lady was lying with her head forward,' McCubbin recalls. 'It was the only way we could make it work. And one of the sisters was sitting in the back left-hand seat assisting her. The other was kneeling on the right-hand seat beside me, leaning over the patient's head giving whatever assistance she could.'

> **'When the baby's born on the aeroplane . . .' the doctor began, giving instructions.**
>
> **'Bullshit, mate: a bloody baby's not gonna be born on my plane,' McCubbin protested.**

Halfway to Darwin just over Maningrida, the baby popped out. 'And, of course, there was bugger all room, so the girls wrapped her up in a space blanket.'

'Hang on to this, will you?' A nurse passed a swaddled bundle to McCubbin. The young pilot was left to nurse the baby for the next hour as the sisters attended to the distressed mother. As Darwin airport approached he handed the bundle back, returned to the controls and landed. Met by an ambulance, mum and baby were whisked off to Darwin Hospital.

In 2003 McCubbin received an invitation from Darwin: the baby he'd helped deliver wanted him at his 21st birthday party.

*

Fishing trawlers would congregate in Blue Mud Bay, near Groote Eylandt, where there was a popular though rough bar where trawler workers drank. One of these blokes had been drinking, dived into the water off the front of the trawler and failed to surface.

It took the authorities a day to reach the scene to investigate and another two days to locate the body. A crocodile had taken the body seconds after the man had dived in and had wedged its prey up underneath the mangroves to soften him up. Tim Travers-Jones was tasked with transporting the remains to Darwin. He had a ghastly few hours putting up with the smell of the decomposed corpse in his Cessna 206.

Tim McCubbin also had a memorable Groote Eylandt prawn trawler story. A worker had been involved in a gas bottle explosion on the boat and had lost a couple of fingers and suffered an eye injury, requiring a medevac to Darwin. McCubbin parked out the front of the little shack that stood in for an airport terminal. The patient, dosed up on morphine, walked over to the Cessna, his hand wrapped up in bandages and a patch over his eye. He was carrying a foam Esky.

In 2003 McCubbin received an invitation from Darwin: the baby he'd helped deliver wanted him at his 21st birthday party.

'Mate, you got a six pack for the journey?' McCubbin joked. With his good hand, the bloke flicked the thing open to show his four fingers and thumb sitting on top of the ice. The boys on the trawler had salvaged them.

The bloke had a tiny piece of metal from the gas bottle in his eye, and the problem with getting him to Darwin was pressure. If McCubbin climbed to a normal altitude atmospheric pressure would decrease, making the eyeball expand and pushing the metal further into his eye, so to minimise the pressure changes McCubbin flew as low as possible: at about 1,000 feet all the way to Darwin.

McCubbin bumped into the same guy some years later. 'Mate, how's the fingers and the eye?'

'Oh, great, mate. I can bend them just enough to hold on to a can.'

'So, what about your eye?'

'Oh, it's a bit dodgy, have a bit of trouble focusing, but when I'm pissed it's as good as gold.'

*

McCubbin tells a story to illustrate that local medical care in places like Groote Eylandt could be far from adequate. The wife of Groote's local ambulance driver had been semi-conscious for three days, and although the island doctor had told her there was nothing to worry about the ambo remained worried. When one of the more experienced medical nurses, Elaine Heineke, came in from Gove to do her regular clinic, he pleaded with her. 'Can you come into town and have a look at my wife?'

Ten minutes after she had examined the lady, McCubbin received a message relayed via the Groote Eylandt refueller: 'We're going to Darwin. Make sure your aeroplane's gassed up, we'll be there in ten minutes.' The nurse had realised the woman likely had encephalitis, a potentially lethal brain infection.

'We raced her to Darwin as fast as we could. Unfortunately, she never recovered, winding up in an almost vegetative state.'

*

Mike Cottell explains that the community's money from government benefits and mine royalties was pooled. He recalls having to fly community members in the Kakadu district backward and forward all day to attend a funeral. One particular lady, 'Betty', was the money keeper. When Cottell needed a flight paid for he would see Betty and she would indicate who to take, open her purse and pull out $500. Cottell's eyes bulged when he realised her purse held over $20,000.

'Coffin charters' involved returning a deceased Indigenous body to their own community. When the state paid the deceased was interred in a simple purple chipboard coffin. The operation meant pulling the seats out of the Cessna 206 to fit the coffin, which depending on the weight of the deceased could be up to 90 kilograms.

> **'Coffin charters' involved returning a deceased body to their community and it was not uncommon to be returning a coffin from Darwin for a ceremonial burial.**

It was not uncommon to be returning a coffin from Darwin for a ceremonial burial. Jerdo Jerdan needed to fly a deceased Aboriginal to his native country near Timber Creek, so two of the Cessna 206 passenger seats needed pulling out so he could lay the body down on the floor of the cabin. Airborne at 9,000 feet, Jerdo glanced around. To his alarm the dead man, still in the body bag, was sitting upright. Jerdo's skin went cold and the colour drained from his face. He radioed Katherine: 'I think he's alive!'

Back at base the team were laughing. Most of the Cessna's were not pressurised, so gas in the corpse could expand as the air pressure changed. Differential pressure in a body at that altitude causes the torso to lift if laid with the head at the rear of the plane.

A similar thing happened to Shayne George, causing a body to move and bump around in the coffin. Shayne had been prepared, but this time there were relatives of the deceased on board. 'They were petrified,' Shayne recalls. 'They wanted to jump out.' Without any stewardess to help him, it took all Shayne's effort to talk the alarmed relatives down and get them to return to their seats.

*

At Timber Creek, Jerdo had landed with his coffin. The Elders who had come to collect the body insisted the plane be smoked out to rid it of evil spirits before the body was removed. No one had informed Jerdo of this ancient ritual, but the Elders would not be swayed. The risk of setting the airplane on fire was alarmingly high, so Jerdo had to think fast. He reached for the aluminium tray that contained the plane's cleaning kit in the rear of the plane. Setting up the tray on rocks in the cabin, he held them back as he added some leaves, sticks and a firelighter. As the leaves started to smoke, he looked around nervously at the tribal elders.

'Is that good?' They nodded in assent, vanishing with the body.

Shayne George experienced similar issues returning a body to Groote Eylandt, where the locals all jumped the low perimeter fence with burning pieces of timber to smoke out the plane. With a couple of hundred gallons of fuel in the wings, Shayne had a difficult negotiation.

*

Two of Gordon Ramsay's first few flights were coffin charters. The first required returning a corpse to the mission outstation near Hodgson Downs, owned by the famously grumpy Bevan Gitsham. Ramsay was instructed to buzz the community by flying low on arrival so they would know to meet him at the airstrip. He followed his instructions and landed, but a half hour passed and no one came to meet him. It was stinking hot, and the mission was too far from the strip to walk. It was heading towards dark and Ramsay needed the body out of his plane.

On the side of the strip were some empty 200-litre Avgas drums. Ramsay rolled three of them up beside the plane, and by pushing and shoving manoeuvred the coffin out onto the first drum. By rolling the back drum to the front repeatedly he was eventually able to get the coffin onto the edge of the strip, before returning to Katherine.

A Tillair pilot needed to be able to problem solve.

*

Tim McCubbin recounts a charter from Gove to Lake Evella airport, transporting the community engineer and town clerk. As they landed another operator's plane was on the tarmac, returning a dead body to the community. As was the custom, the whole community had turned out to smoke out the aeroplane.

McCubbin suddenly realised his passengers had bags of alcohol with them, ready to smuggle into a dry community. 'You can't take these out. If so much as one of those bottles clinks together, you'll be in the shit – and I'll be in even more shit because the aeroplane will probably get confiscated. What's going to happen is you're going to get off and I'm going to fly all this stuff back in to Gove. At a convenient time, I'll bring it back out.'

As it turned out the community took the body and dispersed, so McCubbin reluctantly agreed to let his passengers offload their alcohol. 'Don't you ever put me in the situation where you've got a bloody aeroplane with bags and bags of grog. It's a big no no.'

*

Left: Coffin charters were not uncommon for Tillair pilots.

When Tilly bought Tennant Air in 1982, Gordon Ramsay and Barney Milosev relocated there to start operations with a six-seater Cessna 310 as well as the Cessna 206, the Duck. Barney recalls: 'We used to do a mail run once a week. Tillair also had an agreement with Tennant Creek's small hospital to be on call 24 hours a day for medical evacuations and hospital transfers to Alice Springs and Darwin . . . We had a pager on our belt clip.'

When it went off, Barney would ring the hospital for instructions. The nurse would let him know when the patient would be arriving at the airstrip, and Barney had to hightail it to the strip, ensure the plane was refuelled, the engines warmed up and all checks done.

He had one call-out to Mungabroom Station for a child who had a nosebleed that couldn't be stopped. Based on the verbal report, the Tennant Creek doctor made a call. 'If we don't pick him up now he's going to die.' Mungabroom Station was at least familiar to Milosev, being one of the Barkly Tableland mail-run stops. However, it was after dark and the Mungabroom Station airstrip had no lights, not even flares, which contravened air-safety regulations for night-time landings.

'Doc, you sign a letter saying that it's a mercy flight and I can break every rule in the book,' Milosev advised. With the signed letter, Milosev was given permission to complete the mission. Instead of flares, Milosev radioed ahead so the owner could place one vehicle at either end of the runway.

'Shine the headlights in the direction that we're coming from,' Milosev instructed. It was a pitch-black night but pretty much flat country, so there was no chance of running into a mountain in the dark. If Milosev set his direction carefully and calculated likely flying time, with luck he would pick up the headlights on the strip as he came closer.

*

In Tennant Creek Tilley had negotiated for his team to do any local medevac work, which meant pilots like young Peter Davies needed to be on standby at night in case a call-out came through. Some of these night flights were pretty challenging. One night Davies recalls a call came in from Brunette Downs Station: a worker had suffered serious head injuries after being kicked in the back of the head by a horse. There was no moon up, so the sky was pitch black. The locals called such conditions a 'dark hole'.

By the description that came through on the radio, the bloke's injuries were so bad that waiting until morning was not an option. The medical team made a decision: they needed to get him into Tennant Creek hospital. Davies was told to strip out the Cessna 402 and that the on-duty doctor and two nurses would be at the Tennant Creek strip within twenty minutes.

At Brunette Downs there were two runways, a long one and a short one. The cockies had lit the short one using car lights, with one vehicle at each end. 'The equipment on board would help you but you [were] pretty much just looking out the window,' Davies recalls. 'It's pretty flat around there, so you're not going to hit a hill, but actually getting the aircraft on the runway: it's not easy.

'I was a young punk then. We just wouldn't do that sort of shit now,' Davies admits.

"Pilots & Personalities"

MAKING THEIR MARK ON KATHERINE

In time Tillair was able to acquire a Regulation 203 supplemental licence approval, which allowed them to carry passengers to a schedule and publish the routes while not holding to the same standards as a large commercial airline. For the department, the choice was to either give Tillair this lighter standard of regulation or have no operator on these remote routes.

These regular passenger transit routes required Tillair to carry safety cards in each seat pocket, and the pilot would give a quick briefing on operating the doors in an emergency prior to take-off. These ticketed routes used a Cessna 402 or 404 twice weekly. Two routes used Katherine as their hub: Katherine–Yarralin–Wave Hill–Kalkgurung–Hooker Creek and Katherine–Ngukurr–Numbulwar–Groote, while a third departed from Alice Springs, taking in Yulara, Docker River, Giles and Kintore before returning to Alice Springs.

To Ron Hoenger, Tillair had enormous potential: he wanted to see Tillair planes across the entire country, but one of the key barriers was customer service in the skies. 'The young Tillair blokes, they didn't think about what they were doing apart from building up hours. They weren't cowboys, but they just . . . weren't customer oriented.'

Hoenger gives an example. He was in the front of a Cessna Conquest with a young Tillair pilot, and the pilot needed to descend to land at Tennant Creek. 'There was a whole heap of cloud a couple of thousand feet below us. We're screaming down at the maximum speed the aeroplane could go and I'm looking at the pilot and thinking, well, are you going to slow down or what?

'Anyway, we enter the cloud and the aeroplane goes bang, crash all over the place. That's the thing that scares people in aeroplanes, [the] turbulence,' Hoenger explains.

*

On a Friday late afternoon in Katherine after work the Tillair pilots would gather in the office for drinks. Tilley would send the most junior boggie out with $10 to buy hot chips from the Ampol station. The employee who made the biggest mess that week had to buy the first carton of beer.

Above: The whiteboard would be full of charters from the week prior.

Top left: (L-R): Peter Quinn, John Marchant (Marcho), Jenny Tilley perform in a charity event for the Katherine School of the Air 1983
Top right: (L-R) Penny Tilley; Ron Hoenger; Jenny Tilley; Terry Ey; Scott Tilley, Alan Chatfield (Chatty), Peter Stocks (SOMF) celebrating a birthday;
Left: CLP progressive dinner (L-R) Peter Stocks (SOMF), former Chief minister Paul Everingham, Gordon Ramsay (Gundy) Mar 1984.

The whiteboard would be full of charters from the week prior: pilots doing multiple trips, aeroplanes being swapped. One pilot would rub out the board and John would put up the work pre-organised for the next week.

'I'd say to them,' recalls Tilley, 'all right, everyone look at that. Is there any way we can work a back charter like . . . drop off and then shoot this far and pick up another?' The young pilots might offer a suggestion. 'Then I'd say, okay, if we do that I'll have to ring the government department and say, "Look, we had a bit of a hold up. Would you mind if I didn't pick you up until 14.00 instead of 12.00?"'

This meant Tilley could assign just one aircraft call-out for two jobs. 'You could work out where you could have a saving and

make more revenue for the same amount of time.'

Often, recalls Peter Quinn, 'Tilley would say: "Gee, I've never seen it that quiet. It doesn't look good. I hope I don't have to let anybody go." That was his way of saying . . . Don't ask for a pay rise guys, you might lose your job.'

*

There was a disco every weekend at Katherine's Crossways pub. Even there the Tillair pilots hung together, standing around talking about aeroplanes. Jerdo and Mike Rees went on their first Saturday after arriving. All the meatworkers were propped up on the bar like crows on a fence and the girls were on the other side of the room. Jerdo and Mike walked up to a few good-looking girls

'How 'bout a dance?' suggested Jerdo.

'Ah, go and get f'ed,' the girls snarled back. Their boyfriends were staring from the bar.

Amused, the two lads decided to really stir up the locals. 'Let's get up and dance together.'

*

Recalls Barney Milosev, 'When we had days off we would come into the office because . . . we didn't have air-conditioning . . . We

Tillair sports day L-R: Andrew Hocking; Maurie Guerie; John Tilley; Grant Gumley; John Torr: Paul Grant: Brett Miller; Mark Jerdan: Mike Lucas: Ian Paige; Shirley Hussie, Milly Goodings

couldn't afford to run it, [so] we'd sit in the air-conditioned office and we'd ... drive the bus, load the aeroplanes. So we lived our job ... We were a really close community. We all worked together, looked after each other. We went out together.'

Barney would go water-skiing for the weekend at Lake Argyle, 500 kilometres west near Kununurra, with Rosemary and her husband Terry Ey, the Katherine police sergeant, who invited the guys to accompany them. Tilley would either lend them an aeroplane to fly there for the weekend or he'd give them one of his Budget franchise rental cars.

'We would eat, drink, sleep and water-ski ... spending time on one of the islands in the middle of the lake. And then we'd drive back and be back at work again. We were one big family.'

Milly Goodings recalls: 'We had to make our own fun. A lot of us were young, and while we worked hard we also played hard. Plus being in a small remote town in the heat, most of us drank beer. I remember we had a progressive dinner [and we] hired a bus to transport everyone to the location of each course. At the first location, the beer had not yet arrived. There was only Long Island Iced Tea cocktails, so everyone drank that. Most of us didn't realise the alcohol content. By the time we got on the bus the beer had arrived, but by then everyone was very merry, singing and carrying on.'

*

Each year Katherine hosted an annual frog race, the Croakers Cup. In 1982 the Tillair entry, Hop Harrigan, took out the major prize, but there were other distractions too. Since the mid-1970s the town's annual carnival weekend had attracted close to 1,000 locals and tourists into town to celebrate.

At Katherine's first carnival the organisers had cast around for ideas that might provide some novel excitement for tourists on top of the standard bull-riding and camp-drafting demonstrations. Two motorcycle enthusiasts had suggested they ride a dirt bike across the bottom of the Katherine River, complete with scuba gear and a 5-metre snorkel. After much experimentation one explosion, one fire and one complete engine rebuild, their machine was ready. The bike apparently made it halfway across the riverbed before hitting a dumped refrigerator.

By 1982 there were plenty of young Tillair pilots based in Katherine, and that year five of them decided to put on something much safer but with an enhanced visual thrill. The plan was a group flypast over the main street of three single-engine 210s and two Cessna 310s in a loose spearhead formation, then follow that with a single-plane flypast one by one. Despite none of his boys having any training in formation flying, Tilley was happy enough with the plan.

> **At Katherine's carnival the organisers had cast around for ideas. Tillair's pilots came up with a plan of a group flypast over the main street in a loose spearhead formation**

The three 210s went first, followed by Tilley and another pilot each flying a 310 behind. The idea was that each aeroplane would break off and fly low over the Katherine River bridge then flat out down the main street jammed full with 1,000 people. Each of the single-engine planes flew down one by one with chief pilot John Marchant in the lead and Keith Tym in the other plane, buzzing down to an altitude of just 400 feet.

(L to R) Local policeman Terry Ey, pilots Grant Coleman, Alan Chatfield & Rosemary Ey.

Then it was Woodgreen's turn: he broke off and swooped low. Woodgreen recalls: 'We were so low that we had to pull up to go over the light posts. I was maybe fifteen feet above the ground.' His mate was close behind, his younger brother in the passenger seat. Because the twin engine was going so quickly he worried he was going to catch up, so as the bridge approached he broke away. 'I was pulling around to the right and . . . was pulling around to the left, and then we rolled out and we were flying directly towards each other.'

The pair passed so close they could see each other's eyes. The crowd screamed, loving the theatre of the moment. As the seven pilots flew back towards Tindal the fun continued. John Marchant started a dogfight. 'He comes up behind me and he's going on the radio. Click, click, click, click, like machine-gun fire shooting you,' Woodgreen says. The game was on. The pilots took sides, pretending to shoot each other down.

Unsurprisingly, the daring town flypast made the local papers the next week and came to the attention of the aviation regulator in Adelaide. Aviation regulations allow for planes to fly no lower than 1,500 feet above populated areas. Geoff Browne grounded Woodgreen for a week, demoting him to boggy: he drove the Tillair minibus and loaded all the planes.

Browne urged Woodgreen to apologise to Katherine's mayor; however, Tilley had heard the gossip in town. The carnival had put on an aerobatic plane display prior to the Tillair show. All the locals thought the Tillair show by far the best part of the day, and everybody was raving about it. Given not one local complained, Tilley vetoed the idea of an apology to the mayor. 'We're just going to keep quiet.'

Tilley did receive a stern letter from the civil aviation authority, but he pacified them with an assurance that it was a once-off misdemeanour and would never be repeated.

'In a court of law,' one of the culprits surmises, 'at 400 feet you could argue you were at 1,500 feet. The crowd are looking up. It's subjective.'

*

In Katherine, recalls Ian Paige, 'We weren't getting paid a lot of money, so we used to go in after hours sometimes and ring our families from the office.' However, Tilley used to sit and go through his monthly phone bill, and if he saw an evening call he'd ask himself: 'Would I be ringing Adelaide at 7.00 at night?' He'd ring the mystery number and ask who he'd called. 'Oh, you're Ian's mum and dad, are you?'

Recalls Paige, 'Tilley might then speak to them for an hour about what we were doing. Then he'd charge us for the phone call we made to home. It cost him twice as much as that because he'd talk to our parents for so long along the way.' However, Tilley never let money go by.

Paige had been back working in Katherine for a few years as a relatively senior pilot and he and Leanne had spent $50,000 on a Katherine home. One night at about 8.00 pm he took a phone call for a medical evacuation. He jumped in the car and sped to the airport to warm up the aircraft and meet the medical team, but the local cops pulled him over en route and booked him for speeding.

YOUR ARSE IS SAFE WITH TILLAIR

'Oh, that's pretty tough, guys. You know, I'm going out to save lives.'

'Oh, well, you know, it doesn't matter. You still got to comply with the speed limit.'

Paige decided if he was going to get booked then his mates, the local doctor and nurse, should also. 'Well, don't stop now. You've got the doctor and the nurse coming. You can get all three of us.' Despite the fines, the doctor and nurse thought the prank amusing. 'This is the sort of things we did to each other,' Paige explains.

Paige and the medevac team were back in Katherine by 1.30 am. A half hour later, Paige's phone rang. Oh, not another one, I'm exhausted, he groaned to himself. It was one of the guys in Alice Springs. 'What are you doing answering the phone?'

'Well, I'm on medical standby and I've just done a medical.'

'You've been transferred to Alice Springs. We need you endorsed on the Conquest urgently. Be ready at Tindal airport at 6.00 am tomorrow, there'll be a plane to pick you up.'

Paige grabbed three hours' sleep, threw some things together, kissed Leanne goodbye and was gone. It was three weeks before he had a spare day to fly back to Katherine, pick up Leanne and their possessions and return to Alice Springs. They never saw their Katherine home again.

(L-R): Shirley Hussie (Shirl); Ted Landy; Paul Mann; Anne Diepold; Shayne George

ACQUIRING CHARTAIR

Brian Smith, an ex-SAATAS pilot, ran a similar bush operation to Tillair called Chartair, which was based out of Alice Springs. The business had a travel agency at the back of the Telford Alice Hotel and owned the Alice Springs Travel Centre, which competed with Ansett, TAA, the tourist commission and the Central Australian Tours Association. However, with regard to charter work, Chartair had most of the business out of Alice Springs, including three mail runs – south-east, north-east and north-west – and a north-west settlements service to the mission stations of Ernabella (now known as Pulatja), Fregon (Kaljiti) and Amata. This work serviced patients coming into the Alice Springs health service as well as the occasional school teacher, operating under a long defunct Department of Transport Regulation 203.

With about a dozen staff, including ten pilots, the business was robust, but by 1982 Smithie wanted a change. Running a charter business was non-stop, and Brian was a hard drinker and had blood-pressure problems and his wife Sue wanted out of Alice Springs – and Tilley was again ready to expand. He saw the tourism potential of the region.

Part of the attraction of the Chartair purchase was the access to run sight-seeing flights to Ayers Rock and the Olgas. Tourists could

Chartair's shuttle bus

in the early 1980s board a scenic charter and land on a gravel strip under the shadow of the jaw-dropping Uluṟu. On some long weekends, Chartair pilots took 700 tourists for 25-minute scenic flights over the unique landscape.

Over the previous decade it had become clear that unstructured tourism near the base of Ayers Rock was having detrimental effects on the environment. A Senate select committee had recommended the removal of the rock's airstrip, along with all infrastructure. Instead, from 1982 the Territory government commissioned three competing hotels and a new airstrip to be built at Yulara at a cost of A$130 million.

For Tilley, this timing was an opportunity. The resorts builders, Yulara Development Company, were unlikely to fancy the scheduled Ansett commercial flight times and, sure enough, the developers wanted a regular 8.30 am charter flight from Alice Springs for its staff. Tilley was only too happy to oblige.

'He used every resource he could,' Ian Lucas reflects. 'Ansett's rent probably paid the mortgage for him.'

The acquisition suddenly doubled the size and number of Tilley's routes. When his chief engineer Ron Hoenger learned from a colleague that Tilley had just negotiated the purchase he rang Tilley. Was it true? 'Sorry, I must have forgotten to tell you,' Tilley consoled Hoenger. As an only child, Tilley had never grown used to sharing his thinking with others, let alone his feelings.

*

Chartair ran nine aeroplanes when Tilley bought in, including two Italian multi-engine Partenavia aircraft. Tilley was not a fan, but mining was taking off and the mining companies insisted on using twin-engine aeroplanes to comply with their safety standards. Tilley soon introduced new aircraft into Alice Springs: a Cessna 310R, Cessna 303 and Cessna 206s and years later a Cessna Citation C-550 jet. Some planes inherited from the acquisition such as a Piper Navajo and two Partenavias he sold off.

Chartair ran nine aeroplanes when Tilley bought in, including two Italian multi-engine Partenavia aircraft.

Operations manager Bryce Baud, who had worked for Brian Smith for years, noticed the difference in personalities. 'In Brian's time he would shut up shop at 5.00 pm. Tilley would never do that. He would stay in his office, wheeling and dealing, always looking for an opportunity.' Baud remembers that whenever Tilley was in the Alice Springs office, concerned about catching a cold, he would let fly with a can of Glen 20 to kill any germs before and after a visitor called in.

In the mid-1980s Tilley's self discipline meant he was also off not only grog, but tea and coffee. Instead, Bryce would watch on as he drank hot water with lemon in it.

*

Brian Smith invested his windfall into building a landmark Alice Springs pub. With SAATAS and Connair now out of the picture Tilley saw the opportunity to bed down some of the passengers services that were too small for Ansett to tackle, so he introduced a scheduled regular public transport route that went out to Papunya and Yuendumu. He did the same thing for the north-west settlements into South Australia, though these were later ceded to an Indigenous community operator.

Later, Tilley offered scheduled routes to Kintore, Docker River and Giles, then back via Yulara. Ansett was running its own commercial flights to Yulara twice daily from Alice, but they were ultimately happy to contract out their smaller flight each day to Chartair.

Left: Stephen Marshall & Brian Smith, who sold Chartair to Tilley; Above: Tillair's first International operation - Citation TFY at Jakarta airport 21/09/1985

*

Yuendumu Aboriginal settlement four and a half hours' drive north-west of Alice was already a mail stop on Chartair's twice-weekly mail run. Like Groote, Gove and Numbulwar, Tilley decided to place an aircraft there. Ostensibly, he hoped to replicate the success of the charter work in these outstations, allowing the locals to travel to friends and relatives or to Rabbit Flat roadhouse, 330 kilometres north. Run by the eccentric, rusted-on personality Bruce Farrand, its attraction was that it served alcohol.

The Yuendumu locals were great poker players, recalls Bryce Baud, and might book to travel to another community such as Mount Allen to play. Family groups would travel by air for social occasions.

Under the radar, while Ansett and TAA had exclusive rights to the Alice Springs–Darwin centre run, Yuendumu allowed Tilley to covertly link Alice Springs to Darwin with Tillair flights via Yuendumu, Tennant Creek and Katherine.

With Tilley's purchase of Chartair came pilots, one of whom was John Torr. Tilley decided to test his new employee's loyalty. 'Torr, you're going out to Yuendumu for six months with a Cessna 210.' Torr accepted the move without complaint and lived in a locked-up compound – Torr describes it as a cage – with two nurses and a couple of school teachers. Except for the police and whitefella compound, where pilots, nurses and police alike would regularly get hammered, Yuendumu was a dry community.

There was no access to television signals. Instead, Torr's parents would regularly send videotaped recordings of *Hey Hey It's Saturday* to play on the police station's VCR machine.

Torr would regularly pick up one Indigenous passenger, John Wayne, and his mates from Rabbit Flat to fly them home to Yuendumu. Unfailingly, they would be loaded up with bottles of beer. 'Hey, guys, you know it's a dry mission. You can't bring those back,' Torr would warn.

'Eh, pilot. They be all gone,' Johnny would reply. 'We be drink 'um before we land.'

'No worries.' Torr would get on the HF radio and call through to the police station. 'Am bringing some live ones in, buddy,' he would warn. On arrival Torr would open the cabin door and his passengers would fall out onto the tarmac. The cop would be there, put them straight in the van and lock them up for the night.

'That was how it was done,' Torr shrugs.

At Yuendumu, lining up for the single public telephone was the hardest thing for the young pilot. Instead, phone messages were taken by the local police station. When they wanted a flight the Aborigines knew to come and bang on the door at the front of Torr's house.

*

By 1982 Tillair had grown so fast that new aeroplanes were coming into the business every three months. There were mishaps requiring repairs along with the regular maintenance, and the lack of maintenance staff was becoming a major issue. To help Ron out, all Tillair pilots were expected to spend a day or half a day in the hangar each week, as it was a great way for them to learn more about the mechanics of the machines they were flying. Despite this Ron was drowning. Finding a second qualified engineer to take

Tim McCubbin about to take 402C TZH on her first revenue flight from Tindal in July 1982

some of the load was proving impossible, and Tilley was getting desperate.

When the application from young Adelaide lad Ian Paige for a pilot's job landed on his desk Tilley noted he had trained and worked as an aircraft engineer to fund his flying hours and felt a glimmer of hope. Just months earlier Paige had resigned from his engineering job and proposed to his girlfriend, Leanne; they were already married. It had never been Tilley's policy to employ married pilots, because the need to relocate them to remote outstations at the drop of a hat was problematic. He wrestled with the idea, finally telling Brownie and Hoenger, 'I reckon we can get him up here and give him a job and he can fix our aeroplanes for us.'

At the interview, Paige made it clear that his primary desire was to fly planes. If Tilley wanted him purely for his engineering then he was not interested, but 'If you're looking for a pilot who can fix aeroplanes and be more practical then I'm here for the long haul.'

After the interview Tilley turned to Brownie. 'Well, that didn't work. I didn't get the engineer we needed, did I? . . . But, you know, he was up front. He was honest. I liked him . . . We might give him a go. What do you think?'

Tilley reasoned that Ian's off day could be in aircraft maintenance rather than cleaning, and he promised Paige it would be only one day a week. 'To John's credit,' Paige recalls 40 years later, 'I never spent a second day in the hangar in a week . . . He kept his promise and that's, I think, something that is unique about John.'

Paige had spent five years as an engineering apprentice in Adelaide. His manager there had promised everything he needed to keep Paige happy but with no intention of following through. 'In contrast, John made me twenty promises along the way and he kept every single one of them,' Paige declares. Paige and his young wife moved to Katherine.

There weren't that many jobs in a small town, but she quickly secured a job with the local council. They were anxious that she stay on good terms with her new employer, so if they needed to be posted elsewhere she needed to plan. Leanne warned her husband: 'You better let him know I need to give him two weeks' notice.'

Paige went in to see Tilley, saying: 'John, just by the way, I don't know when you're sending me to Numbulwar, but I do have a wife, you know, and she has a job and she'll have to give two weeks' notice if that's a possibility.'

'Two weeks?'

'Yes, John, two weeks.'

'Good, that's your two weeks' notice today.'

Given most of the young pilots found remote postings challenging, the normal Numbulwar posting was three to six months. However, Ian Paige was different. Stable, dependable, and he had a wife for comfort. Paige could do his own aircraft maintenance so Tilley sent the couple for a year. Leanne did all her husband's paperwork, found work in the Numbulwar shop and then the council gave her teaching work. Ian Paige explains that even whitefellas could not live in such a traditional community 'for a long period of time without having your place'.

Because they were there for a year the local community embraced them. 'I ended up with an Aboriginal last name, which gave me the lineage it needed for us to be able to live there. They take it very seriously.'

'Poison cousins' or avoidance relationships exist in Anindilyakwa culture, where certain people are required to avoid family members or clan. Such rules forbid direct communication, facing each other or proximity. For a woman, her poison cousin or nadija is her son-in-law (her daughter's husband) or the son of her mother's brother. For a man, his poison cousin or dadija is his mother-in-law or the daughter of his maternal grandmother's brother.

Paige and his wife Leanne found themselves soon entwined in these rules. Paige explains: 'One of my wife's good Numbulwar friends used to come and visit us all the time.' Her friend's father was declared to be Paige's uncle. 'This meant my wife's friend was now my cousin. From that moment on I never saw her again. She always left when I came home... It was the most interesting thing to see. We went to certain levels of ceremonies. As I was uninitiated

I could only go to those that could be attended by uninitiated people.'

For the 22-year-old Paige it was 'a tremendous experience. Sitting down on the beach, fishing with the locals, talking with people [who] can remember seeing the first-ever white man.'

*

Paige's flexibility changed Tilley's attitude to married pilots, and Tilley would later admit he had been wrong to only employ single blokes. By contrast, of those who were married he said: 'They're flexible, they're much calmer, they don't get into trouble with the cops at the pub. From now on I think everyone should be married. It's good for them!'

Paige's flexibility changed Tilley's attitude to married pilots and made Tilley realise that he had been wrong to only employ single blokes.

By this stage a bunch of Tillair pilots had girlfriends. John Tilley went out of his way to encourage weddings and was generous with his aircraft. When Barney Milosev was engaged in Tennant Creek, Tilley allowed a Cessna 310 to fly in his Katherine mates for the engagement party. Tilley loaned another two Cessna 210s to bring mates from Alice Springs. When Milosev tied the knot in December 1984 in Perth Tilley did the same thing, flying ten guests in a Cessna Conquest from

Alice Springs to Perth and back, picking up Rosemary and Terry Ey en route.

When Gordon Ramsay was married in Darwin Tilley put on two planes from Alice Springs and one from Katherine to fly Gordon's guests to the wedding. As a wedding present, Tilley gave the newlyweds a dishwasher for their new Alice Springs home.

For Peter Quinn's Adelaide wedding, Tilley put on two Cessna Conquests to fly guests in from Alice Springs. 'I might have shamed him into it,' Quinn laughs. 'He was a hard ass but absolutely generous.'

Bryce Baud recalls Tilley giving permission for three or four planes to take out some of his staff to enjoy the famed Birdsville Races one year. This remote country race weekend was even then notorious for attracting huge numbers by air and road. 'Just look after the aircraft and don't get into any trouble,' Tilley growled.

As a sweetener, Baud had arranged to take some paying passengers. Dozens of light aircraft flew in on the Friday afternoon, and a temporary air traffic control tower was set up to handle the volume. The famed Birdsville pub is in walking distance from the airstrip, and Baud recalls there being hundreds of patrons drinking, swarming around boxing tents, chatting and carousing. The blokes took their own Eskies and slept in swags under the stars. The racetrack was further out of town so all those who had arrived by light plane would hitchhike there, jumping in the tray of flat-bed utes.

> **Bryce Baud recalls Tilley giving permission for his staff to take three or four planes to enjoy the Birdsville Races one year.**

Baud recalls one of their passengers being arrested on the Saturday night in possession of a bong and marijuana. The next day, a Sunday, he had to front the local magistrate, who fined him $50. The bloke did not hesitate in asking for his bong back.

There were other occasions when Tilley let his young pilots borrow planes to let off steam at the popular Mataranka rodeo, the Kalkaringi cricket match or the Timber Creek races, where horses raced around a track that disappeared in clouds of dust.

*

> **John would always give you an aeroplane if there was one available. His standard phrase was "I'll send you the bill on Monday."**

Tillair pilot Tim McCubbin's girlfriend's best friend came up from Melbourne to visit them in Alice Springs with her partner. McCubbin asked Tilley if he could borrow a plane to show them Ayers Rock on a quiet weekend. 'Yep, no worries,' Tilley replied.

'John would always give you an aeroplane if there was one available. His standard phrase was "I'll send you the bill on Monday."'

On the Saturday morning McCubbin was about to head out to the airport to borrow the plane when Tilley called again. 'Oh, I've had to send the 210 out, but you can take the twin engine.' McCubbin cannot recall ever paying for an airfare while working for Tilley. His boss would ask him, 'Where are you going?'

'I'm going down to Melbourne to see Mum and Dad.' McCubbin would turn up to work the next day and there'd be an Ansett ticket for a Katherine to Melbourne return. 'So while he never paid me the award . . . it never bothered me,' McCubbin admits.

At another time Tilley had just bought a Cessna Citation Jet. McCubbin needed just another two hours' flying the Citation to be fully endorsed when a client booked a charter to Maryborough in Queensland. McCubbin and his girlfriend had booked their leave at Hamilton Island, so McCubbin asked if he could fly the jet over to Maryborough with a co-pilot. From there he could take a commercial flight to Hamilton Island.

'Yep, no worries.'

> **Whilst Tilley did not pay the award, his generosity was well know amongst pilots.**

Next morning, waiting at the Tillair office were not one but two tickets: one for Jenny to fly from Alice Springs to Brisbane and Hamilton Island and one for Tim to fly from Maryborough to Brisbane, Hamilton Island and then back to Alice. 'We worked very hard for him, but he was well aware of that.'

Katherine office worker Rosemary Ey recalls that in 1981 she and her policeman husband Terry were booked to fly to Alice Springs for Christmas with relatives. Two days beforehand, Ansett cancelled the flight and Rosemary despaired, then her boss rang her with an offer. 'If you can wait until Christmas morning I can divert the south-east mail run pilot to Alice after he's dropped a Christmas ham to Hodgson River station. You'd just have to give him a bed for the night.'

Young Tillair pilots were working thousands of kilometres away from their families, so were often unable to make it home for Christmas or birthdays. Instead, John and Jenny Tilley would step in to host a Christmas at Pandamus for all the staff needing to stay on duty. Hosting birthday parties for his young charges was also a regular occurrence. In October 1985 Stuart Palframan flew in from Groote Eylandt, where Tilley put on a 21st birthday celebration for him, Shayne George and Mark Diamond at Pandamus. Tilley gifted each of the young pilots with a pewter tankard.

Shayne George, Stuart Palframan & Mark Diamond celebrate their 21st

NEAR MISSES, MISHAPS AND A WIN

'They used to do some crazy things, risky things,' Scott Tilley says of the young Tillair pilots, 'and they were encouraged in risk taking by Dad as well. If the weather was a bit iffy but you needed to make a delivery you'd push a bit harder, but then you'd have a story about a near miss you'd had.'

The experiences of some of the young pilots were pretty frightening. Engine failure in a single-engine plane was a pilot's worst nightmare. not to mention the huge cost of replacing them – the engines, not the pilots. Mark Jerdan was in a single-engine aircraft one night 100 miles north-east of Katherine, bringing back a load of bananas from Gove. He was halfway through a position report to Darwin flight services when the engine stopped.

'Standby,' he interrupted his radio report. The escarpment below would be an issue as the aircraft descended. Jerdo was resigned to having to land; he just didn't want to hit a hill the wrong way. He managed to get the engine to run intermittently on one magneto and climbed about 300 feet before the engine cut out again. The pattern repeated. The problem was there was no airstrip with runway lights between his current position and

Katherine. Flying at around 1,000 feet with terrain either side of him, Jerdo could just make out the road below and followed it. It would do for an emergency landing if it came to that.

He somehow reached the Katherine airfield, and Tilley was there to meet him in the company minibus. Before unloading the banana load he handed Jerdo a six pack of beers. Jerdo's legs felt like jelly. 'Fuckin' just tried to kill me,' he swore. He turned away from his boss, suddenly noticing the plane's fuselage was covered in oil. 'Holy shit, did I forget to put the oil cap on?' Mark was thinking this might be his fault, but when he checked the cap he found it was secure.

While they unloaded the bananas together, Jerdo polished off another four beers to calm his nerves. The next day, engineer Ron Hoenger called Jerdo in to show him what had happened. Planes have two magnetos to spark, one on either side of the engine. One magneto had cracked the housing and was leaking oil, and it had thrown off a bit of steel that bounced off the top of the engine cowl and damaged the other magneto. It was a freak accident.

*

When he was in his early twenties in 1982 Peter Quinn also survived a Tillair engine failure, this time in a Cessna 404 regular passenger route out to Roper River and Groote Eylandt. Quinny and his nine passengers heard a loud 'bang, bang' sound and a shudder. Quinn's adrenaline was high as he shut down the engine; thankfully he was flying a twin engine. As the propeller stopped turning his passengers squinted out the window aghast at the stationery propeller. The young pilot did his best to calm them and radioed ahead to Katherine to get the fire department out to meet the plane.

Tilley had heard the radio call-out. He dropped everything and drove out to the airport to meet his young pilot. 'Come inside, you probably feel like a stiff scotch,' he grinned to the pilot. This was Tilley at his most caring.

*

John Torr also experienced an engine failure. He recalls one of the oil-rig workers he had picked up wanted a turn at the controls, so once they were airborne Torr gave him the controls. Meanwhile, Torr busied himself with catching up on paperwork. Suddenly, one engine cut out. Torr grabbed the controls from the rigger, wound in the rudder and feathered the propeller. 'I requested descent . . . In those days you don't say too much [to air trafic control] cos it's only going to cost Tilley money . . . So down I came, requesting to fly a lower and lower altitude.'

'Everything okay, JT?' came through the query on the radio.

'Nah, I've lost my right engine,' Torr finally admitted. Down at 4,000 feet, Torr calculated he could make it to Alice Springs on the one engine, but then 100 kilometres out the remaining engine started to overheat. He would have to make an emergency landing in Hermannsburg, 50 miles from Alice.

'I knew I'd get back in time for the happy hour . . . We were bulletproof in those days. We were Tillair pilots, for god's sake.'

*

Not long after Hoenger had started in Katherine in 1981 a new Tillair pilot, Andrew Downing, took up a local property owner and his son in a Cessna 206. The task was dingo baiting, which meant very low-level flying. Young Downing was used to flying a Cessna 172, in which you can select both tanks so fuel is fed from both. However, the Cessna 206 and 210 had a fuel tank on each wing, so the pilot must feed fuel from one tank or the other with the aim of regularly switching between them to keep the fuel load balanced.

The young guy forgot to transfer his fuel feed, and suddenly the single engine spluttered to halt. With more altitude Downing could have selected the other tank, hit the boost pump and the engine would start again, but at 100 feet he was too low. All Downing could do was attempt an emergency landing, during which one of the wings hit a tree. Downing was not wearing the shoulder harness of his seatbelt, and as the plane crash landed his head slammed on the dashboard. Both he and his two passengers needed medical evacuation to Darwin as all had suffered significant head injuries.

The airplane had to be written off. When Downing recovered from his injuries he continued to suffer blackouts. His flying career was finished.

*

Another Tillair pilot, Andrew 'Lurch' Hockings, was ready to land a Cessna 310 at Groote Eylandt when his indicator light for both the nose wheel and the two side wheels failed. Unsure of whether they were down, he turned around and returned to Katherine, radioing ahead to emergency ground services. On overflying the aerodrome he received a welcome message on the VHF radio: the wheels were down, so he was able to make a safe landing. The waiting ambulance, police and fire brigade were all sent home.

For a single-engine plane without radar, pilots had to ensure they could see the ground at all times. However, the wet season came with a tonne of rain, storms and lightning and visibility could be shocking. Such conditions failed to stop intrepid Tillair pilots.

Mark Jerdan remembers one time the authorities were anticipating an impending cyclone. During the wet season turbulence is an everyday event, and on this day it was severe to extreme. Tilley had received a call-out: three blokes in Maningrida were prepared to pay charter rates to get out before the cyclone hit and Tilley wanted Jerdan to do the pick up.

'Shit, John, do these blokes know there is minimal probability I'll be able to get them? And if so, they need to know they are paying regardless?' Jerdo queried. Tilley knew Jerdo would take on the challenge. He had enough fuel to get from Katherine to Maningrida and back if the Maningrida landing had to be aborted.

Turbulence associated with wind shear is the most dangerous issue for light aircraft in a storm. Sometimes there is no way a pilot can control their altitude in such conditions; they just had to ride with it. Such turbulence could rip a plane to pieces, requiring great care not to overstress the aircraft. In the tropics thunderstorm cells tend to have far greater vertical reach than on the east cost of Australia and it was not uncommon to have storm cells reaching up to 50,000 feet.

On this day the conditions were bad, so Jerdo climbed to a safer altitude above the clouds. On a standard instrument approach Jerdan could not get in to Maningrida as there was no visibility, so he had to think fast. He flew out over the water. His Cessna had an instrument called a radio altimeter, which works directly off ground-surface feedback and gives an accurate height calculation. Jerdo was able to turn towards land, descend to 250 feet below the clouds and circle the approaching airstrip before landing safely. The three workers were mightily relieved, but their problems were not over.

'Fellas, strap in, you're in for the ride of your life,' Jerdo warned them. His passengers looked at their pilot wide-eyed. 'On the return to Katherine we were in some pretty serious weather,' Jerdo recalls. Landing back in Katherine at dusk, Jerdo badly needed a few drinks to debrief.

*

Left: Six TILLAIR planes waiting for assignments at Tindall airport

Keith Tym was based in Katherine on medevac duty when he received a call-out to evacuate a woman from Hooker Creek to Katherine Hospital. It was close to midnight and the wet season, and an electrical storm with regular lightning strikes had hit the district. To make matters worse, the larger Tillair plane with radar navigation was out of service so the only choice was the Cessna 210, which only had an automatic direction finder (ADF) to help with night navigation.

Tym explains: 'If you were close to Tennant, Groote, Gove, Katherine or Alice there were beacon aids. Apart from that you were looking out the window or following ADF.' However, electrical storms played havoc with these devices, making the navigation aid flip around and follow the lightning. Moreover, the Hooker Creek airstrip was unlit, so flares would need to be put out by the local policeman. Despite the dangers, Tym decided to chance it. He recalls having to dodge lightning strikes en route.

*

Tim McCubbin was flying into Kalkgurung, an Aboriginal community south-west of Katherine, when he blew a tire on landing. The mishap also took a chunk out of the wheel rim. He sent a message back to Katherine telling them they needed to send Ron Hoenger down and that he needed to bring an entire wheel, not just a tyre and tube. The message must have been lost in translation, as Ron turned up with only a spare tyre. Being the middle of the wet season, Ron refused to overnight in Kalkgurung while a new wheel was dispatched, so they improvised.

Fortuitously, McCubbin had gone looking for the missing wheel rim and managed to find it on the airstrip. Locating some tape in the plane's medical kit, they re-attached the metal piece to keep the wheel balanced and inflated the tyre as little as possible, so it didn't put too much pressure on the Band-Aid solution.

'We flew back to Katherine in the dark,' McCubbin recalls. 'There were thunderstorms everywhere, but we managed to dodge them.'

*

In 1982 Ron Hoenger recalls going out to Tilley's Pandamus home one Sunday to borrow his tractor.

> **Tilley took the hard punches well and didn't blame people for making mistakes**

'I've gone and done it,' Tilley confessed.

'What's that?'

'I've bought a prop jet.'

Hoenger was confused: he was already looking after an enormous fleet of Tilley aircraft. 'Ah, who's going to look after that?' he quizzed Tilley.

'We'll cope,' Tilley said, brushing him off.

It was brand new; Tilley had borrowed US$1.2 million to buy it. Conquests were a pressurised ten seater turbo-prop plane with the ability to handle rough landings, and Tilley had bought the second one to come into Australia. To give his pilots some exposure to the new aircraft, Tilley suggested John Marchant fly it on a medical clinic run to Waterloo station near the Western Australian border, but when Marchant taxied out on the Waterloo station runway to come home the plane's undercarriage fell into a soft bull-dust hole, damaging not only the engine but the propeller and landing gear door. He radioed into base in Katherine, and Hoenger and Tilley flew out to inspect the damage. Marchant was in tears.

Pilot Hugh Cohen forgot to lower the wheels of his Cessna 421c URT as he made a landing in 1986;

Tilley walked over to Marchant, putting his arm around him. 'We pushed it too hard, old mate, didn't we?' was all Tilley said, in an instant taking away all the anxiety that had choked up the young pilot.

Another engine and propeller would need to be flown out and a tractor would need to tow out the fuselage. 'Tilley took the hard punches well and didn't blame people for making mistakes,' Hoenger observes.

*

At one stage a pilot was flying out a bunch of executives in a Cessna 182 to inspect a mine, but he became confused as to his whereabouts out in Arnhem Land. Flight services had a propensity to take over if a pilot was unclear of their position. 'The worst thing you can do is get on to Darwin,' Tilley confesses, 'but this is what the guy did. Every five minutes Darwin would radio "Are you visual, are you visual?" It scared the shit out of him.'

The pilot found a flat area to make an emergency landing nose up, but it was soft soil and he forgot to put the wheels down. The plane was stranded. Tillair's team could have flown out and picked him up, but the authorities refused. Instead, both pilot and passengers had to sit out there overnight while the aviation authority organised for officials from Brisbane to fly through the night to the remote site in their twin-engine helicopter.

'The bureaucracy and the crap you've got to go through!' Tilley shakes his head. 'Because that's what the book says. They've got no fuckin' idea.'

Ironically, on their way back to Brisbane one of the twin engines in the authority's own chopper failed.

*

On another occasion Hugh Cohen was booked to fly the Northern Territory chief minister from Darwin to a remote country airstrip near the Queensland–Northern Territory border in a Cessna Conquest. A high-performance aircraft, the Conquest cruises above the clouds.

Descending through the cloud cover, Cohen followed the usual protocol of overflying the station homestead to alert the owner to come out to the airstrip. After landing Cohen went to the back of the aircraft, lowered the stairs and announced 'NT Chief Minister Everingham' to the waiting cocky. Everingham put his hand out to greet his constituent, but was cut short.

'Well, that's all well and good, mate, but you're in Queensland,' the cocky drawled. Cohen was at the wrong property: he had overshot the Northern Territory station by at least 10 miles.

*

In 1982 Tilley and his wife Jenny decided to totally rebuild Pandamus using a rammed-earth technique. They had been visiting Margaret River in Western Australia and seen the results in striking homes there. Their new house would be in the same position, but they decided to build the foundation slab 18 inches above ground level. Years later when the Katherine River flooded, their decision paid off.

The next year Tilley drew Kiwi in the Territory's famed Tomaris Sweep, a Melbourne Cup charity sweep in aid of the Rotary Club, chaired by Tilley's mate Reg Laurie. Kiwi was first past the post, and Tilley's win was a whopping $15,000. Laurie thought it would be a good opportunity to arrange for the media to photograph

Tillair's first Conquest was badly damaged after falling into a soft bull-dust hole on the remote Waterloo station

Tilley with his winnings, in sequential $1 notes, before taking the cash back and replacing it with a cheque. However, Tilley liked the idea of a stash of notes and he asked to keep 1,000 of them: a memento he has never parted with.

> In 1983 Tilley drew Kiwi in the Territory's famed Tomaris Sweep, a Melbourne Cup charity sweep. Tilley's won and took home a whopping $15,000.

The windfall was enough to pay for the foundations for their new home. The Tilleys enticed two Western Australian chippies with the right experience to come to Katherine and supervise the build. A tall Chinaman based in Alice with a firm called the Great Wall Company did the structural work, and an expert in the rammed-earth process, Graham Bambridge, shifted to Katherine with his family for some time to supervise. During the build the Tilleys lived in a demountable temporary dwelling, a caravan and a makeshift sleep-out close to the building site.

The rammed-earth structure was advertised as naturally cooling the interior. With wide verandahs around the house, John decided not to install any air-conditioning: it was another expense he could do without. Regardless, when the temperature soared in summer Jenny would take her pillow and sleep outside. It was two years before John gave in.

*

At one time Peter Davies recalls there was a report of an emergency position indicating radio beacon (EPIRB) going off out near Victoria River Downs. Back in Katherine, a call came through from the emergency services: could Tillair provide as many planes as possible to join the search? It would mean a handsome day's charter earnings for Tilley so six young Tillair pilots, most of them with few flying hours, were called in to help. The emergency services were co-ordinating the search via HF radio, a difficult job at the best of times.

Davies says the search and rescue documentation described how to do a search in remote country. 'We didn't really know what we were doing; we were just reading it out of the book. So we're all doing our search patterns . . . We can hear the beacon, we can't

hear the beacon, and reporting back. Anyway, we just cannot find it . . . then all of a sudden it cuts out.'

Finally, Geoff Browne twigged as to what was going on: someone had crashed a Victoria River Downs chopper and decided not to report it to emergency services to save the hassle of an investigation. Instead, the VRD chopper manager had simply sent out a truck to pick it up and bring it back to base, but the trouble was the EPIRB was still going out. 'We were tracking this moving target for hours on end,' Davies says, shaking his head.

*

In 1987, 21-year-old blond, blue-eyed Stuart Palframan was scheduled to make his first south-east mail run out of Alice Springs in one of Chartair's Cessna 210 aircraft. The route took in nine remote cattle stations stretching south into the Simpson Desert, and Palframan was assigned two 'scenos' – typically tourists – to tag along. This time one of them was journalist Jenny Brown.

'There are two types of pilots in the Territory,' Palframan told the journo, 'those who have been lost and those who are gonna get lost.'

By 1984, Tilley had brought in specialists from WA to totally rebuild Pandamus using a rammed earth technique to cool the interior

Landing at the fourth station on the route – Tieyon, just over the South Australian border – the Cessna came to a jarring halt. Palframan swore quietly and bolted from the cockpit: he had forgotten to put the wheels down. The plane had belly landed, and the propeller was bent up and the engine silent. Mortified and mute, Stuart turned an ashen grey. He returned to the homestead for a cup of tea and phoned Alice Springs: 'Ace to base. Report of a mishap.'

Ron Hoenger flew down to assess the damage, while another Chartair pilot, Robert Young, followed in another Cessna 210 to continue the all-important mail run. On arrival, Hoenger silently stared at the fuselage and shrugged; he had seen a couple of wheels up landings already. 'They were inevitable,' he admits, 'because somewhere along the line pilots forget to put the wheels down.' It would require bringing a few guys down the next day, jacking the plane up to install a new propeller and put down the wheels.

When Tilley heard about the accident he was steady as a rock. 'Don't worry about it. We'll get it fixed.'

Back in the air in the replacement Cessna, they headed for the next station, Lambina. The strip looked rough from the air and, sure enough, the landing was hairy. When they inspected the damage they found the front suspension had collapsed. This time Robert Young made a radio call: 'Ace to base, come in, over. Report of a mishap.'

Ron and Stuart picked up the call while airborne. They diverted to Lambina to pick up Young and his two passengers, leaving a second broken plane on the airstrip. Running out of daylight and with a passenger still to pick up, the remaining five stations on the run were abandoned. There was always tomorrow.

Tillair pilots' relative inexperience could be costly. Hoenger calculated that the day's mishaps and putting on another aircraft the next day to finish the mail run would cost the business thousands

Left: Stuart Palframan forgets to put the wheels down at Tieyon station
Above: Much to their embarrasment, Stuart Palframan & Robert Young's mailrun mishaps were featured in a Good Weekend article in 1987.

AYERS ROCK

With the acquisition of Chartair came not only charter flights to Ayers Rock and Yulara, but an established scenic flight business taking tourists over Ayers Rock, the Olgas and sometimes Kings Canyon. Tilley's pilots, usually aged around 23, needed to not only fly and refuel the aircraft but maintain records, book in Alice Springs maintenance checks, manage the finances and tout for business from the busloads of tourists and coach drivers. The work was challenging to say the least, and many had stories from this time.

By 1984 the authorities were building both the massive Yulara Resort and the new Yulara airport, and the transition to the new facility promised to be a headache. Tilley had for years relied on his young charges doing just three- or six-month stints at the rock, but now he needed a reliable pilot who could stay on for a year to work through the complicated transition. Ian Paige, with the support of his uncomplaining wife Leanne, was the ideal solution.

Paige recalls the posting was demanding. During the peak season from April til October there could be three pilots working, but in the off season there wasn't officially enough work to justify more than one.

Tilley had the rights to the refuelling contract for all aircraft, but it was located at the old Ayers Rock airstrip. The problem was

CHARTAIR's scenic flights were hugely popular yet dwarfed by the massive Ayers Rock standing 348m high, with a total perimeter of 9.4 km.

all scenic flights had to come and go from the new Yulara airport 25 kilometres away, which meant Paige had to juggle 'two aeroplanes, two airports, a Tarago to pick up the passengers and a ute'.

Paige might have passengers needing to be picked up from Yulara and someone's plane to be refuelled at Ayers Rock. Leanne would pick up the passengers from their hotel and drive them to Yulara airport. Paige would put her in the back of the aeroplane, take off with the passengers and drop Leanne at the Ayers Rock strip. She would race over to refuel the second plane. Meanwhile, Paige would complete the 20-minute scenic flight, return to the Uluru strip, pick up Leanne and continue to the new Yulara airport, where Leanne would drive them back to their hotel in the Tarago while Paige checked in the next group.

Paige recalls: 'I never had the right aeroplane or the right car at the right airport at the right time.'

In time it suited other airlines such as East-West to refuel their 20,000-litre Fokker Friendship tanks at Yulara en route from Tamworth to Perth, so Tilley had to employ a full-time refueller at Yulara and invest in fuel trucks and equipment. However, once the Transport Workers' Union figured out the Yulara refueller had to be available at 2.00 am to refuel the East-West jets, they insisted Tilley pay him penalty rates. Suddenly refueller Mike Pittman became Tillair's highest-paid employee.

*

At the end of every day Tilley's pilots had to ensure one of them was at the viewing platform at sunset with a clipboard to take bookings from the busloads of tourists for the next day's scenic flights. Because sunset flights were also popular, Ian Paige explains, 'We sort of needed to be in two places at once. When there [were] a bunch of pilots it wasn't a problem, but in the quiet season it was.'

On one such evening Paige was manning the business solo. He was running late after landing a scenic flight and had only minutes to get out to the viewing platform a few kilometres away, so he parked the aeroplane on the strip, jumped in his car and raced out to the viewing platform. While there, Paige noticed a bit of lightning out in the distance towards the airport but thought nothing of it. I'll go back out to tie the aeroplane down and put all the covers on, he thought to himself.

On his return to the airstrip, 'I came around the corner and there's three wheels sitting in the air,' Paige says, wincing at the memory. A storm had come through and blown the aeroplane upside down, smack on its roof.

While Tilley was disappointed, he never challenged Paige's judgement. 'You have to get the bookings. I get that. You didn't know what was coming.'

Left: By 1986, TILLAIR had upped its marketing of profitable secenic flights with glossy brochures. Above: Iain Paige finds his Chartair Cessna flipped over after failing to tie it down

166　AYERS ROCK

In 1983, CHARTAIR's scenic flights were still using the airstrip metres from the majestic Ayers Rock (207 UAA)

Although Tilley suggested tying the plane down would be a good idea, 'He got the whole thing. He understood it wasn't through me just being slack,' says Paige. 'It's the fact I was juggling so many things. I made a call and it was the wrong call. I think that's an unbelievable thing [given] the disruption that caused and the cost. I mean, he was insured, but the reality is it was written off. There was no repairing it.'

*

There was one tourist Ian Paige sold a scenic flight to that he regrets. It was a 30-something woman who really wanted to go up but admitted she was a very anxious passenger. 'Well, that's cool. You'll be fine,' Paige reassured her.

One of ten tourists on board, as Paige checked his instruments the woman buckled in and confessed again: 'I'm really, really nervous.'

'You know, you shouldn't be. There's nothing to worry about.'

Ten seconds after take-off, as Paige was climbing at 200 feet, the woman 'lost it', unclipped her seatbelt, wrenched the door open and was about to jump out. It was only the efforts of a quick-thinking passenger beside her that prevented a disaster: he managed to grab her and dissuade her not to jump. Paige made a rather quick turnaround, landed and took her off the plane 'an absolute wreck, quite incoherent', Paige recalls. From that moment, when people confessed they were nervous flyers Paige took them very seriously.

*

Richie Cornish was one Tillair pilot who once drove trucks in Western Australia's salt mines, 'A really, really nice salt of the earth guy,' recalls Tim Travers-Jones. Richie was flying a Cessna 207 on half-hour scenic flights under Tim's supervision.

Tim recalls one time Richie took off to go out over the Olgas and up to Uluru, but about eight minutes later Tim noticed him coming back in to land. 'He was joining the downwind part of the circuit at high speed,' Tim recounts. Out on the tarmac with the refueller, Tim could hear the engine screaming. 'Then the engine stopped and it was just gliding, and then, as he turned to come in to land, it went again. Bang, bang, bang. Silence.'

On the aircraft's final approach the sound changed again: 'Beep, beep, beep, beep.' The plane sat dead still on the middle of the runway.

'We literally hand pulled it off the runway,' Travers Jones recalls, 'which you couldn't do now. You'd be arrested.' They parked the plane, disembarked the passengers, put them in the bus and refunded their money. The refueller stood under the wing, climbed up onto the ladder and opened the fuel cap.

'So, what's the story, Ferris?'

'Tim, there's nothing in this tank except the maker's name on the bottom of it.'

Richie had overlooked refuelling the aircraft.

*

At the end of Paige's Uluru posting he was told to report to Alice Springs so he could fly the bigger planes. 'I packed up all my gear. I arrived in Alice Springs and I get myself all unpacked,' Paige recalls.

A week later, Tillair's Alice Springs operations manager asked him: 'Didn't they tell you you're transferring to Tennant Creek?'

'Oh, right.' Paige and Leanne reloaded their gear into the car, drove the six hours to Tennant Creek and unloaded. Four days later they had the last box unpacked when came a message from head office in Katherine.

'Where are you?'

'We're in Tennant Creek.'

'No, no. Did no one tell you you're supposed to be in Katherine?'

Paige had to pack his gear for the third time. 'It took me three weeks to go from [Uluru] to Katherine via three stops.'

*

Two years after Tilley's takeover of Chartair, two of his young pilots realised that unlike most of their colleagues they would not have a straightforward progression into commercial aviation. In was 1984; Ian Lucas and Chris Dawes were each in their mid-twenties. To get into the airlines you needed not only flying hours but to have decent grades in maths and physics in high school. Ian's other passion besides flying was music: he was an accomplished pianist. Without any science subjects, even getting a commercial airline interview was unlikely.

'I was a bit of a lemon,' Lucas realised.

> **Two of Tilley's pilots started their own charter company, having realised they would not have a straightforward progression into commercial aviation.**

Chris Dawes was colour blind, a condition that affected his ability to fly at night. 'I don't think I'm going to make it. It's been recommended that I start a business on my own,' Dawes confided in Lucas.

'Well, we should do something,' Lucas agreed.

They registered their own charter company, focusing on scenic flights for tourists over Uluru and the surrounding attractions. 'John didn't see it coming,' Lucas admits of his former boss. 'We got to the point where the licence was about to be issued before he found out.'

Lucas got home one day and the phone was ringing. He knew what was coming; it was Tilley. He gave Lucas what for, finishing with: 'As of now you haven't got a job.'

Chris Dawes had been about to pull out of the venture, but now that Lucas was out of a job both were determined to make a go of it. Tilley 'virtually forced our hand', Lucas reflects.

They leased a Cessna 206. The trick to success was winning the business from the tour buses that came through on an almost daily basis, so Lucas and his mate made a point of chatting up every tour bus driver and convincing them to sell-in their passengers. The driver would collect the monies, $20 per passenger, pocket a 10 per cent kickback for themselves and even complete the passenger manifest lists for each flight.

'It helped us get things done promptly and efficiently. The coaches were the main part of our business,' Lucas admits. 'It was a good system, because they [the drivers] pre-sold the flights. We were opposition to him but he was so smart, Tilley, that he owned the fuel bowser at [Uluru],' Lucas explains, 'so he controlled the fuel. We initially couldn't buy fuel from him; we had to buy 200-litre fuel drums and pump it into the plane ourselves with a hand pump.'

Ultimately, Tilley realised Dawes and Lucas were not giving up so he might as well sell fuel to them. 'I was actually taken

172 AYERS ROCK

Accounts all caught up, empty trays. Back row (L-R): Rosemary Lincoln, Cathy Gleeson, Shirley Hussie, John Tilley; Front row (L-R) Melanie Brown, Milly Goodings

by surprise when he did that because he had no need to,' Lucas reflects. 'He's just making his $0.10 a litre out of what we buy.'

Tilley's Uluṟu scenic flight work went from being a Chartair monopoly to being shared with his ex-employees. Competing against Tilley inspired Lucas to work that much harder because he knew he was 'up against the best'. Cleverly, the young men even did a deal with the biggest coach operator, APT Luxury Travel, offering them a cut for every APT passenger who took a scenic flight. The operator signed the deal, and Lucas and his mate suddenly had a sizeable market share on a plate and known cash flow to cover their fixed costs.

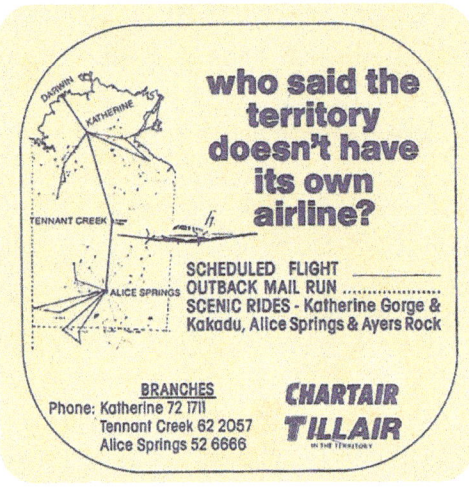

'We worked very hard and we were very successful . . . We fairly quickly had the lion's share of the market . . . because we were 26 up against a guy who was highly successful. We got a lot of sympathy business . . . from people in Alice Springs.'

When the Yulara project was being developed Lucas admits his business also won 'a lot of work that we probably shouldn't have got because people just liked us'. Ultimately, the pair were able to buy two Cessna 206s and a Cessna 402 and leased a third Cessna 206. They even launched a travel agency.

Chartair had the Docker River freight run from Alice Springs, but Ian Lucas came up with an idea that Tilley would have been proud of. He approached the Aboriginal community with a plan to save significantly on their perishable freight costs: instead of air freight the entire 600 kilometres, Lucas offered an overnight refrigerated road freight to Uluṟu then a 45-minute flight from there. Overnight freight gave this solution a 200-mile head start compared with the flight from Alice Springs. It was a very good deal for the community.

'Despite now being competitors, John and I had a cordial relationship,' Lucas admits. 'He just liked what I did . . . John once said, "Well, you showed me how to operate in that environment."

He was quite gracious. He was the sort of guy that when you had him on the ropes, he admitted: "You guys are doing it well."'

However, three years on Chris and Ian Lucas were exhausted. As young blokes they and the Chartair pilots all played hard after working long hours. 'We'd had an incident with a fatigued bus driver carrying our customers having an accident,' Lucas recalls. 'We became a little bit concerned: what if the same thing happened when we were up in the air?'

In 1987 they approached the successful Roger Leach, who owned Central Australian Helicopters. 'Would you like to buy us?' Leach asked them to name their price. 'It was good money and set us both up very well,' Lucas admits. 'It was almost sold too quickly.'

> **Tilley noticed the Ayers Rock scenics were hugely profitable, so he made sure to take his young pilots out for a celebration dinner.**

For years Tilley had been rostering young twenty year olds to Uluru to compete with Air Services Ayers Rock, to little effect. With Lucas gone, perhaps there would be a new opportunity? Soon after Leach took over, John Tilley decided to deploy one of the newer nine- passenger Cessna Caravans in his fleet to see if tourists might be won over. He asked Tim Travers-Jones and his mate Stuart Palframan if they would agree to a back-to-back outstation posting, going straight from Groote Eylandt. It would mean postponing their endorsement on a twin engine.

The pair agreed, and as Travers-Jones recalls, 'We just made it our mission to try and try [to] break the back of the opposition.' It was around the time of Australia's bicentennial celebrations and there were a lot of international tourists wanting to visit the rock.

'We would do sunrise flights and then work all day and then do sunset flights and then we'd go to the bars and drink with the bus drivers and try [to] get them all on side. We ended up changing that business around . . . from very low market share to most of the market. All but the ATP work, who were legally contracted to fly with the opposition.'

Tilley soon noticed the Ayers Rock scenics were hugely profitable, so he made sure to go to Uluru to take his young pilots out for a celebration dinner.

*

By 1984 the Territory's chief minister Paul Everingham had taken a seat in federal parliament[1], which signalled regular charter work from Darwin to Canberra. Tilley's plan was to offer the sleek aircraft to the Territory's politicians. Inside the pressurised turbo-prop twin he had a bathroom installed and a cocktail bar stocked with brandy. Airnorth had a King Air, a much bigger-looking plane than Tilley's Cessnas but more expensive to own and operate. The Cessna was also faster, so Everingham preferred it.

*

Ultimately it was Milly Goodings who became (in Tilley's words) the 'rudder' of the Tillair business. Tilley completely relied on Milly to keep things going from an accounts and administrative level. She was in charge of Tillair's entire backend operations, supervising all accounts and profit and loss reports. These were enormous, given she had accounts to reconcile for seven Tillair bases throughout the country as well as aircraft maintenance divisions in Katherine and Alice Springs.

Milly recruited and trained accounts, reservations and travel agency staff. She prepared and checked invoices, sales returns, creditors and cashbook entries. She oversaw the staff payroll including group tax, payroll tax and superannuation for some 70 staff. Then there were trip revenue manifests, travel agency returns and air ticketing systems reports, including revenue per flight and aircraft, ticket status and statistics for the aviation department.

As the business grew Milly moved into a bigger office and got an assistant. With Tilley away so much, he decided to make Milly sole signatory on Tillair's business cheque account so bills could be paid in his absence. By this stage the pair worked together like a well-oiled machine.

After leaving the business to be with her husband Brad in Darwin for 18 months, on Milly's return she found the accounts were far behind. She organised additional staff and within three months had the business back on track.

---

1 Everingham was elected to the Darwin seat of Jingili in the NT Legislative Assembly in 1974. Just months after being re-elected to the legislature in 1977, he was named leader of the CLP after Letts was unexpectedly defeated in his own electorate. He thus oversaw the transition to self-government, becoming the Territory's first Chief Minister from 1978 to 1984

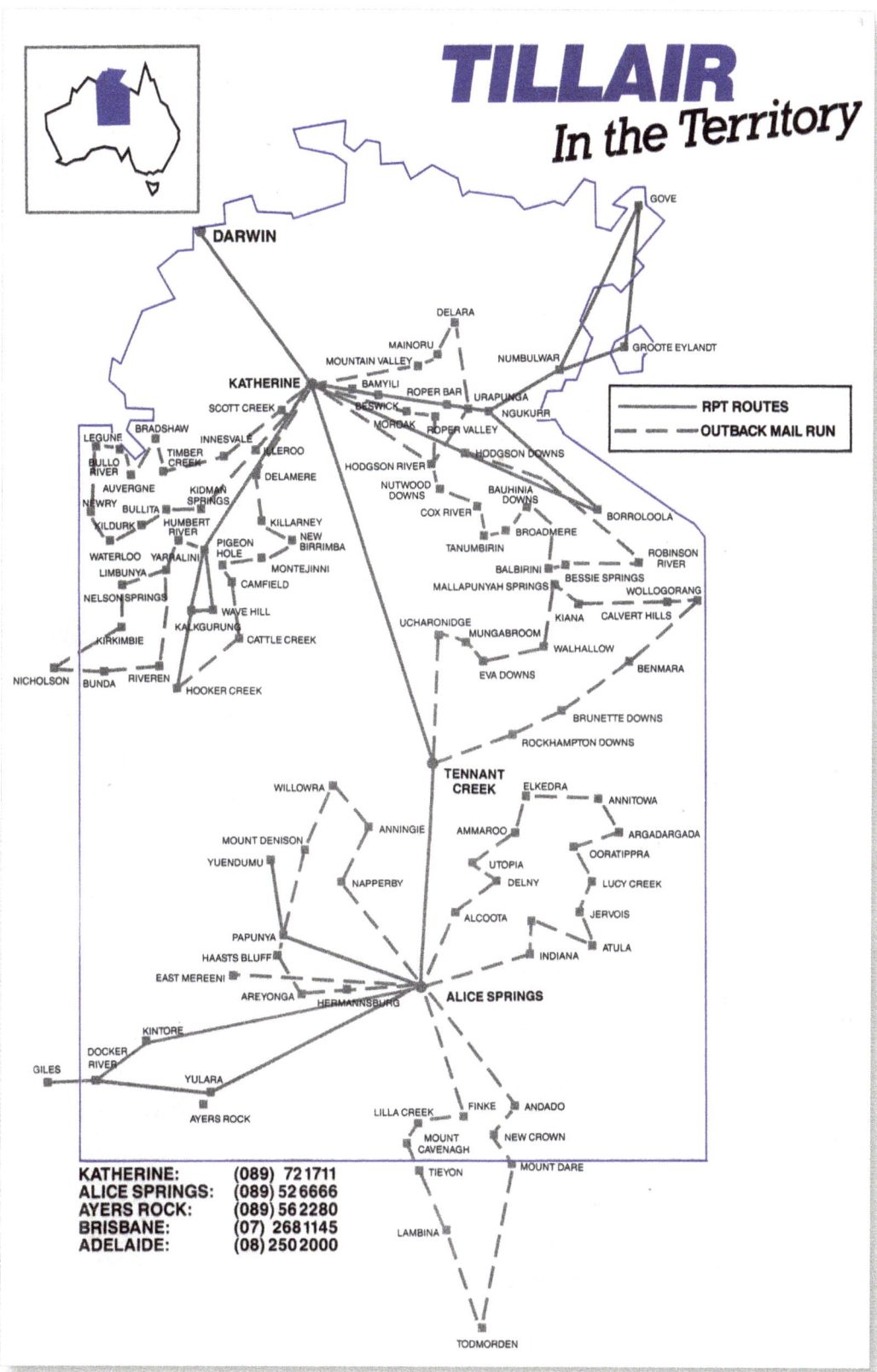

By 1985, TILLAIR had a huge network of both Regular Passenger Transit and outback mail run routes throughout the Territory and into WA and South Australia

NEW PLANES AND HELICOPTERS

In 1984 Tilley created Pro-Air in Adelaide with Erno Sopru as the chief pilot. At the time TNT had a bank-run contract with Australia's major banks to bring in each day's cheques from regional centres to be processed in the capital cities. Transporting magnetic databank tapes and general freight were a part of this work.

In 1983 Tilley had won an important part of this lucrative contract from Alice Springs to Adelaide return, working with TNT Adelaide operative Geoff Lauder. The incumbent, Wings Australia, had been using a pressurised Cessna 421 on the route but their payload was limited, and the Wings flight would leave Adelaide in the morning, fly to Alice and sit there all day in the sun before returning that evening. Tilley had a better idea.

He calculated that his Conquest turbo-props with their 1-tonne payload could be engaged overnight when they would otherwise sit idle. After a day doing charter work in the Alice region, his pilot could spend 30 minutes stripping out the seats, installing cargo nets and load in the TNT freight consignment. As night fell the Conquest could take off for Adelaide at 6.00 pm, offload freight to the TNT vans, load another consignment then return to Alice at 4.00 am.

Tilley purchased this JetRanger 206B TFH for Geoff Browne to fly in 1987, pictured here at Tindall airport

The next year Melbourne was added to the contract. The jet would sit an hour on the Tullamarine tarmac before returning to Adelaide, landing at 2.00 am. Tilley kept a company car and flat in Adelaide for his pilots to use. A replacement pilot would have the plane back in Alice Springs at 7.00 am, where he would re-install the twelve seats ready for a 9.00 am passenger flight to Uluru.

Recalls Tilley, 'I could just see the big picture to give service, to save people time and be more efficient, and that helped TNT and it helped me.' The work gave Tilley a freight contract four nights a week, maximising the use of his expensive Conquest turbo-props.

*

By May 1985 Tilley had also picked up overnight freight contracts from Brisbane to Sydney and Melbourne return. Again, he made sure the Conquest was well utilised. Like the Alice Springs TNT work, this meant the pilot would swap out the freight nets and barriers on arrival back in Brisbane, replacing them with passenger seats in readiness for general charter and mining crew flights during the day.

> **By May 1985 Tilley had picked up overnight freight contracts from Brisbane to Sydney and Melbourne return. Again, he made sure the Conquest was well utilised.**

It was this regular freight work that encouraged Tilley to consider investing in a Brisbane-based air charter business. He wanted one that already had lucrative contracts with the booming Queensland mining industry. Sure enough, Tilley found this in Transair, an operation whose purchase immediately gave him night-time freight and charter work up to Cairns and a reason to base a few more pilots in both Queensland cities. The acquisition came with two TC-690 Aero Commanders. Transair had the TNT contract, meaning regular night work stopping at Mackay, Rockhampton and Cairns to deliver the newspapers and whatever

else was in the load. When Peter Davies was doing this route, he recalls it being every second night. 'But we were young punks . . . happy to have the job and getting the hours.'

Mike Lucas was allocated to the night freight route up and down the east coast; it departed five nights a week. He recalls there was a regular freight run up to Townsville transporting newspaper printing plates so the national newspapers could be printed there overnight.

The key problem for Alice-based chief engineer and general manager Ron Hoenger was it meant he was constantly on call in regard to mechanical issues. If the phone rang at midnight or 1.00 am he knew it was a Melbourne problem, and if it rang at 3.00 am or 4.00 am he knew it was an Adelaide issue. Often Ron would have to talk the pilot through getting the aircraft back to base. 'Then I'd go out to the office all day to deal with other problems. It took a huge toll.'

The Cessna planes would arrive in crates from the USA. At Bankstown, mechanics would assemble the planes. There was profit in not only the aircraft sales but the spare parts. Tilley had for years been sourcing engine spare parts through the Sydney-based Cessna dealer Rex Aviation as well as its Western Australia equivalent. Even more economical was sourcing parts in bulk direct from the US through Steve Bach, the brother-in-law of Darwin aviation leader John Hardy.

However, sales of Cessnas were at this stage dwindling, and in 1985 Tilley saw a new business opportunity: he joined a syndicate to buy Rex Aviation, the Sydney Cessna dealership. This team held the business for three years, even taking over the Singapore-based dealership for some time, although the Asian operation focused more on supplying jet aircraft and spare parts. Both were not huge profit centres but, again, the cash flow was useful and they made a profitable sale of the business to Peter Abeles in 1988.

*

The centre run was a ticketed regular passenger transit service between Alice Springs–Tenant Creek–Katherine–Darwin. For

years Ansett and TAA had been running unprofitable 70-seat Fokker Friendships in parallel on the route, but the aircraft were far too large and expensive for such a low-volume route. Since the Territory had gained its independence from Canberra the federal government had cut back enormously on subsidising remote air routes, so in 1981 TAA had pulled out. Ansett rebranded its jets as Northern Airlines and used the larger F-28s, but they remained an expensive plane to run and still failed to turn a profit.

In September 1983, concerned to maintain air services to remote areas dependent on aviation, federal aviation minister Kim Beazley had announced increased subsidies for air services in remote areas, including the Northern Territory. It was a much-needed win for Tillair, especially given their costs had increased.

In 1984 Ansett contracted Tillair to run its Cessna Conquest every other day on the route. Tillair pilots would overnight in Darwin's Poinciana motel, a step up from the Leprechaun Lodge, and next morning would do the run in reverse. For the young Ian Paige, the Conquest was 'the biggest aeroplane ever built. It's my first turbine aeroplane.' In his mind it had even more status as he was flying in on a commercial route for Ansett. 'I have made it to the big time. I can't believe it,' Paige recalls.

However, for the passengers used to the far larger Fokkers the eight-seat prop jet appeared alarmingly small. Paige recalls at Tennant Creek one passenger came out onto the tarmac, looked around for the Fokker friendship, stared at the Conquest and cried out: 'I'm not flying on that piss farting little thing.' She turned around and went back to the terminal.

Paige admits, 'I went from . . . here I am at the top of my game to a passenger refusing to get on my aeroplane because it was too small.'

*

Ultimately, Tilley had four Conquests, the busiest of which was flying 100 hours weekly and with a maintenance service in Alice Springs every weekend.

At one time Paige landed a Conquest in the middle of the Tanami Desert on a charter. The HF radio was playing up and he had to get a passing Qantas aeroplane to relay a message. 'I'm requesting an airways clearance climb to 33,000 feet.'

The Qantas captain was stunned. 'What? You should be climbing to 5,000 feet. Now, son, you've got to help me out. What aeroplane takes off in the middle of the desert and climbs 3,000 feet higher than I can get in my jumbo? What am I missing?'

*

In about mid-1985 Hoenger made plans to travel to the US with Tilley on a further purchasing spree, this time to purchase another Cessna Conquest to service the growing need on the centre run. British Aerospace had got wind that Tilley was in the market for small jets and pushed hard to sell him and Hoenger their new nineteen-seater Jetstream 31. Such a sale would give the remodelled plan some much-needed endorsement, but Tilley and

> *In mid-1985 Hoenger made plans to travel to the US with Tilley on a purchasing spree,*

Left: Three of Tilley's Cessna Conquest II 441 Turbo Props (KDN, TFB & TFG) at Alice Springs airport

Hoenger knew the aircraft lacked the power required to cope with the Territory's extreme heat. Besides, even a nineteen-seater was more capacity than the centre run could handle. In Tilley's view the outback population would need to double before a plane of such size would be viable for the remote towns he serviced.

Hoenger recalls, 'We went down to Sydney to get on the flight to United States, and these guys actually chased Tilley up and got hold of us at the airport. We're waiting to depart, and one guy is talking to Tilley and the other guy is sitting there talking to me.'

'Look, can you do something?' the Jetstream executive pleaded. 'We find Tilley so hard to deal with: he just won't commit. Can you say something to get him to commit?'

'No, I can't make him commit. He's the bloke [who] makes the decisions and you still got to overcome the problem with the engine. The engines aren't powerful enough for the heat.'

With regard to Conquests, Tilley was keen to purchase but he needed Ron to assess the mechanicals. Their US buying trip took them from Boise, Idaho to Denver and Grand Junction in Colorado; to Fort Lauderdale, Florida, Kansas City, Columbia, Ohio and then on to South Carolina and Dallas, Texas. Whenever they learned a plane had been in an accident it was ruled out. At motels around the states, Hoenger would arrive to find messages about aircraft issues from Tillair staff back home.

One aircraft they took for a test flight in Grand Junction, Colorado during winter. The pilot was reluctant to take the plane up to full power, but Hoenger laboured the point and the pilot increased the power. As he did so, one of the other dial readings shot up so Hoenger knew there was a problem. When they landed he took the pilot aside. 'I don't think you've changed the seals in the engines.' The pilot swore under his breath. On all other counts the plane was good, and Tilley rubbed his hands together: he was ready to do a deal. Seeing that Hoenger had identified a fault that would be costly to fix, Tilley leveraged this to screw the owner down on price.

The fly in/fly out work for mining companies was another one of Tilleys conquests.

*

A further reason for another Conquest was the fly in/fly out work for mining companies. From 1985 Tillair were doing this for miners and engineers based at a remote minerals exploration site, the Granites gold mine west of Alice Springs. At the time the mine was in the exploration phase before becoming fully operational.

Ron Hoenger recalls the mine airstrip was often a problematic landing, and that there were times when pilots would fly out and the weather was so bad the mine couldn't be located. 'The weather in the territory when it's bad, it can be really bad, with really low cloud,' Hoenger explains. Tillair's Cessna Conquest could be used in bad weather but they must fly high at 30,000 feet, well above any low cloud. 'And if you can't get below that level and see the ground then you can't descend. That's a safety rule so that you are 1,000 feet above the highest obstacle or terrain in a given area.'

Quite often a pilot would go out there and have to turn back and come home. The mining group were never very happy about it, but there was no alternative. 'We thought we were going to get the ongoing FIFO contract when the mine became fully operational,' reflects Ron Hoenger. It was worth a lot of money and the Conquest turbo-prop they had just purchased from the US would be ideal, but a few incidents in the months ahead worried Hoenger.

First, on a regular pick-up from the mine site one of the passengers arrived ten minutes after the rest of the tiny planeload. The cocky Tillair pilot turned to the late arrival. 'In future will you make sure you're on time?' the young pilot snapped.

The latecomer turned out to be the operation's general manager, nicknamed 'Colonel Sanders'. Given they were paying huge amounts for a charter plane and pilot to operate to their needs, the GM was furious. The mine manager's wife, Cindy, was a matronly sort who when you met her you knew you had to respect her. She had charisma. On Friday afternoons when the mine flight returned to Alice Springs, Cindy used to come out to the airport to meet her husband and drive him back into town.

Hoenger recalls: 'We had put in our bid for the contract and Tilley kept saying to me, "Have you heard anything? Have you rung anybody up?"'

'They won't talk about it, John. You know, they're just playing their cards close to their chests.'

The weeks dragged on, then John Tilley was in Alice one day. 'Have you heard any more about the contract?' he asked Hoenger.

'No, nothing's been said.'

'Oh, well, I'll sort this out.' Tilley grabbed a plastic shopping bag and half a dozen beers and trotted off into the mine manager's office on a Friday afternoon to have a chat.

'He came back to me and he said, "Well, that was no good. There was nobody there."' A week later, Hoenger ran into Cindy en route to meet her husband.

'That John Tilley: who does he think he is! Why, does he think we can be bought with a few beers and a plastic bag? If he thinks he's getting a contract, he's got another think coming.'

'First one of our pilots insults the general manager, then John insults the wife of the boss,' Hoenger reflects. He could not bear to tell Tilley.

Weeks later the Perth-based SkyWest won the contract. Not only had SkyWest committed no faux pas, but in its tender they had assigned the client a dedicated aircraft and pilot to use whenever they liked. 'What really hurt,' remembers Hoenger, 'was that the two engineers who were working for us quit and started their own business to do the Granites maintenance.'

*

By 1986 Tillair's services in the Territory, South Australia, Queensland and Melbourne were averaging well over 64,000 flying kilometres each week. The airline had twenty scheduled Northern Territory services, selling passenger tickets to no fewer than thirteen towns and settlements as well as delivering paying passengers, mail and freight to 47 remote Territory stations. That was a total of 60 runways and landing trips in the Territory alone.

> **By 1986 Tillair's services in the Territory, South Australia, Queensland and Melbourne were averaging well over 64,000 flying kilometres each week.**

The Katherine office itself had twelve administrative staff to manage the bookings, paperwork and accounts. They had outgrown the rabbit warren of poky office space in town, so Tilley moved the office out to Tindal airport. Ultimately, Tilley recalls, 'We had agents at all these remote places.' In 1987 the business employed 58 staff. There were 31 pilots spread across eight bases, including eleven out of Katherine and seven in Alice, not to mention the four based in Brisbane and two in Cairns. There were nine maintenance staff in Katherine and Alice and satellite offices in Brisbane, Alice Springs and Yulara.

> **In 1987 the business employed 59 staff, with 31 pilots spread over eight bases.**

Hoenger admits he never knew just what Tilley was going to buy next. Geoff Browne was keen on a helicopter, so Tilley decided to reward his loyal first pilot. Mike Cottell recalls on one occasion Brownie flew the chopper in, landing behind the Katherine Railway Arcade office. However, he had come too close to the surrounding trees, trimming them with the chopper blades. To rib Brownie, the young pilots put an ad in the Katherine paper advertising a circular clearing service.

Pandamus would occasionally flood, cutting off the road to town, so locals would have to take a tinnie across the floodwaters. Those kids who lived on the Gorge Road might be given the day off to avoid mishap, but not the Tilley girls. At least three times Kate Tilley recalls their dad dialling up Brownie to ferry the girls in the Tillair chopper to school. The trouble with the helicopter was, every time it came into the hanger for a service there were so many moving parts that the bill would be at least $20,000 and take a week. This compared with a Cessna service, which could be done in a day and might only cost $1,200.

Kate and Sarah Tilley remember going up in one of the Cessnas with their dad and a young pilot, the seats all having been removed for freight. Once they were at 1,000 feet the young pilot nose dived and the girls screamed with delight as they floated around the cabin. Another thrill was the pilot killing the engine while airborne.

*

A helicopter was not the only new aircraft on Tilley's shopping list. One Tillair pilot dispatched to Sydney remarked on his return to Ron that he had sighted Tillair's newest acquisition: a thirteen-seat single-engine Cessna Caravan.

'What caravan?' Ron was confused.

'Oh, don't you know about it?'

'No idea,' was Hoenger's terse reply. He rang Tilley.

'Oh, I must have forgotten to tell you about it,' Tilley confessed.

Tilley had purchased the first Cessna Caravan to arrive in Australia. These Cessna 208s would become the most popular workhorse for outback operators.

*

Back on the centre run, Tilley too was struggling to make a profit even with the ten-seater Conquests. Passengers continued to baulk at travelling long distances in such a small jet aircraft, particularly during the wet season. There was a perception, Ron Hoenger explains, that small aircraft were dangerous, not to mention the fact that their cramped interiors made them uncomfortable for passengers. Passenger numbers dropped dramatically, and within just a few months Tillair lost around $130,000. Tilley announced he was going to withdraw from the run.

'Pulling out was a big deal,' Ron Hoenger explains. Tilley was asked on the radio by a local journalist: 'What could make you keep it running?'

'Well, we need some profit, Matt. There's no profit in it.' That was a bottom line for everything Tilley did.

*

One day Hoenger was sitting in a Cessna 210 flying between Alice and Katherine with Tilley. Tilley turned to him. 'You know, we shouldn't do this very often together. If this thing goes down, the whole company goes with it. All the maintenance is in your head and all the businesses in my head.'

It was true: Hoenger did not even have a written inventory of spare parts the business held. He could tell you exactly what the business held, but that was no help if he died in a crash.

Given Tillair's ballooning size, Tilley needed more help with management. A year earlier, with Ron Hoenger threatening to leave, Tilley had instead suggested he simply relocate to Alice Springs and take on the role as general manager there, overseeing engineering and operations. It would give Ron and Ros a new environment and Alice was now the centre of their country-wide operations.

Ron agreed, but it meant Tilley needed another general manager on the ground in Katherine to oversee the financials. Milly Goodings was the obvious choice: she knew the business inside out, but the chauvinistic Tilley wanted a bloke and one with connections.

Wolfgang Ertner's main attraction was he had been an adviser to the Territory government so would surely be useful, given he was pretty well connected to Treasury as an economist and bean counter. Offered a salary more than twice what Milly Goodings was receiving, she had high expectations. The trouble was Wolfgang had no understanding of the aviation industry so was forever asking Milly for advice, then he would take her ideas and claim them as his own. Before Wolfgang, planning meetings had consisted of a beer on Friday nights in the office: it was all over and done with in a few minutes. Wolfgang, however, ensured that at every meeting the attendees were provided a glass of water and a pen and paper.

'We all just choked laughing,' recalls Hoenger. It was a novel approach for this overgrown bush operation.

Tillair had never set budgets, and to his credit Wolfgang insisted the team forecast expenses and income for the year ahead. Hoenger recalls management meetings in Katherine where he and Tilley tried to keep Ertner satisfied.

'We're trying to bullshit how much we spent on maintenance, how much was spent on fuel,' says Hoenger. 'We're just plucking figures out of the air. John's saying, "How much do you reckon we should say for this?"' Wolfgang could not believe it.

Hoenger recounts an incident where a Tillair pilot had flown into bad weather in the wet season. He had been forced down and had to land on a black soil plain. The black soil was like glue, so on landing the aeroplane had tipped over and the passengers and pilot were stranded overnight. At the next morning's office meeting, Wolfgang started to talk about recovering the aircraft.

> 'There are two types of pilots in the Territory,' Palframan told the journo, 'those who have been lost and those who are gonna get lost.'

'Well, can't we just fly another aeroplane out there and get them out?' he asked.

'No, you can't. That's why we're in this trouble, Wolfgang.' It was clear to Hoenger they guy had no practical sense. 'What are you going to do: are you going to get a tank or a bulldozer to go out through the jungle?'

Tillair had to report aircraft flying hours statistics to the aviation department. Wolfgang suggested amending the reports based on pilots logged flying hours, so before he made a fool of himself Milly had to explain in detail why this would not work. She eventually realised that as long as she was there to cover his gaffes John Tilley would never recognise Wolfgang's failings, so she resigned. Some months later Wolfgang was ousted. With Milly also gone, Tilley was forced to employ an internal accountant and two more accounts staff to handle Milly's workload.

TILLAIR 10th Birthday
A SPECIAL KATHERINE TIMES FEATURE

John Tilley presents the Tillair team. Back row from left:- Mark Diamond, Dina Dennien, Gerry ...ck, Leigh Ward, Graham Roberts, Barry Ford, Peter Stendell, Shirley Hussie, Tony Markwell, Greg Harris.
Second row from left:- Stuart Palraman, Mark Morley, Sean Reynes.
Front row from left:- Anne Diepold, Rose Lincoln, Vicki Thomas, Jenny Richards, Kat...

STAFF AND REGULATORY PROBLEMS

The only engine specialist team accredited to do the hot-section inspections of the Garrett turbine engines in Tillair's Cessna Conquests was in Wagga Wagga, meaning the planes had to be sent down each time. By 1986 Tillair had so many Conquests these service costs were skyrocketing. Tilley and Hoenger decided it might be a good idea to build their own engine workshop in Alice Springs, so Hoenger sought out a decent Wagga operations engineer, Ron Rouse, asking if they could meet.

The night after they interviewed him, Tilley and Hoenger went for a drive. What kept playing over in Hoenger's mind were a few strange responses Rouse had delivered. 'Do you want to bring your wife in and we can talk to her about moving to Alice Springs?' Tilley had offered, knowing such a change was a major decision for a family.

'Oh, no, no, she'll be right,' Rouse had shot back. 'Look, she's got a weight problem. She doesn't like to see people.'

Tilley was a bit unnerved. He asked Hoenger: 'There's just something in my guts about this bloke. You get that feeling?'

'Yeah, it's just, he's just a bit unnerving to talk to, a bit of an odd sort of character,' Hoenger agreed, but both knew employing the guy would save them a ton of money. They needed him.

'We put it aside as just being a quirky sort of person,' admits Hoenger. Tillair paid for Rouse's entire family to relocate to Alice Springs. Hoenger said: 'When he moved into Alice, I kept getting these invoices from furniture places for bloody tables and chairs and lounges. I rang the furniture place up and said, "What are you billing us for?"'

'Oh, we got a purchase order for you.'

'No, you haven't. We have a specific purchase order book.'

'No, we've got this order.'

Hoenger soon discovered it was a purchase order book you could buy in the newsagent. 'Ron Rouse was buying all this furniture for his house and charging us. That was never the deal.' Then there were the unexplained absences. Rouse would disappear from the workshop for a couple of hours at a time, so one day Hoenger followed him into town and as he drove to a workshop with a sign out the front: Rebel Rousers. It turned out Rouse had started a car mechanic business and was working on these while he was supposed to be working for Tillair.

Next was the kleptomania. One guy, Dieter, had a catering business in the back of the Alice Springs hangar for all the airlines that came through. He had boxes and boxes of chips in the corridors with no real security. Dieter said to Hoenger one day, 'I keep losing boxes of chips. I don't know where they're going.' It turned out to be Ron Rouse.

Hoenger recalls the first engine that Rouse worked on for Tillair. 'He put it back together and put it in the aeroplane and it wouldn't start . . . I had a feeling something was wrong.' Hoenger asked Rouse to pull the engine out and kept checking on the bloke before he hid whatever was wrong. Rouse had put in one of the turbine wheels backwards, so it was never going to run.

'It went on and on and on until eventually he did work on one engine [that] Tillair freighted to Brisbane, where they put it in one of the Conquests. The engine blew up when they were testing it.'

*

By late 1986 Hoenger was sick of the red tape around maintenance and repairs. He was spending hours on phone calls every day just keeping the fleet in the air and longed not to be harassed day and night. He had become so stressed from battling problems around so many sites he began to suffer anxiety and depressive symptoms. 'It took a huge toll on me,' Hoenger admits. 'I just wanted to find a room in a back corner of some place where I wouldn't have any responsibility . . . I could go to Canberra and vegetate.'

At the Department of Civil Aviation's (DCA) insistence Tilley put on a new chief pilot, Ron Beech, the first time Tilley had installed a senior person who had not been trained from within. Ron was ex-military. Struggling to find work, he had been doing time with a reportedly dodgy aviation outfit in Western Australia.

Once Ron Beech came on board, John Tilley recalls: 'Then the unions realised we had all these aeroplanes with Tillair on the tail flying all around Australia and 50 pilots . . . [They calculated] a fair bit of revenue for the AFAP.' In the eyes of Tillair pilots, the Australian Federation of Air Pilots union was relevant to commercial rather than general aviation. Unlike commercial pilots, until the mid-1980s very few Tillair pilots joined and those who did were almost ostracised.

> **The AFAP wanted control of the industry and its president Captain Buck Brooksbank was tasked with bringing Tillair's pilots into the fold.**

'There was nothing they could do for us to improve our work conditions,' recalls Tim McCubbin. However, the AFAP wanted control of the industry and its president Captain Buck Brooksbank was tasked with bringing Tillair's pilots into the fold. In 1986, while Tilley was away in the US, the unionist hosted a meeting in Alice Springs that advertised free drinks. It was too good an offer for the young Tillair pilots to refuse.

By the meeting's conclusion the young Tillair boys were unconvinced. Brooksbank was 'almost shamed out of town', recalls Hugh Cohen.

A second meeting was called, and this time Brooksbank pointed out that only through joining the union and forfeiting 1 per cent of their annual salary could pilots access loss of income and life insurance. To blokes so young insurance was not a carrot, but Brooksbank had an ace. Unless Tillair's pilots joined, the lucrative shared Ansett routes from Alice to Darwin and Alice to Uluṟu and the TNT freight work would dry up. This equated to valuable flying hours on the Cessna Conquest turbo-props, every Tillair pilot's goal.

Brooksbank refused to give up: Tillair did start losing some of its shared Ansett and TNT freight work. At a third meeting and by then getting the hang of the Tillair culture, the unionist announced drinks would not be served until after the meeting. 'If you don't join the federation then you won't be able to get a commercial aviation job,' he blustered.

Every Tillair pilot signed.

Recalls Hugh Cohen, 'Tilley had to start paying award wages, annual leave and loss of licence insurance.' Annoyed, Tilley was no longer able to offer his pilots free aircraft for the weekend.

> **Tilley had to start paying award wages, annual leave and loss of licence insurance.' Annoyed, Tilley was no longer able to offer his pilots free aircraft for the weekend.**

*

One of Ron Beech's first Tillair compliance concerns was a Cessna 210 with a faulty turn and bank instrument. In daylight hours the instrument's little skidball gears adjust the rudder to get the aeroplane flying straight, but the bank side is only necessary for night flying. The bank part was faulty, so Beech grounded the plane. When Tilley heard he rang Hoenger, who went to Beech to explain that the fault had no effect on safety because this aircraft flew only in daylight hours. 'The regulations state that you must have a serviceable instrument.' Beech would not budge.

The pattern repeated itself, with Beech grounding further aircraft for minor infractions of the regulations. Hoenger had most of the required accreditation licences to sign off on repairs, particularly for the Conquest turbo-props, yet Beech was concerned he was not doing the DCA-mandated post-repair inspections.

Hoenger recalls unionist Bucks Brooksbank ringing him. 'Oh, you know, we're working with DCA to close down operations like yours.'

'He was an arsehole,' Hoenger says, shaking his head. When just two years later the Australian domestic pilots' dispute crippled the AFAP, clearing the way to airline industry deregulation, to Hoenger this was justice. He and his wife took an extended break in Sydney. Hoenger had no real desire to return, such were the headaches, and unbeknown to Tilley he quietly put in a number of job applications, including one to join the DCA.

Meanwhile, with Hoenger away on leave, Beech wrote to the DCA alerting them to his concerns about Hoenger's practices as well as Tillair's aircraft maintenance and documentation. DCA inspector Jim Brenton was quick to arrive in Alice Springs.

Hoenger recalls: 'I got a phone call saying that I should come back because the shit hit the fan.' He flew through the night on the Westwind freight run from Sydney, landing about 7.30 am to meet Brenton at the air traffic control office. Hoenger says: 'Our paperwork wasn't up to scratch. We didn't have the manuals that DCA wanted.' More Tillair flights were grounded.

'This is not going to do my application any good, is it?' Ron grunted. He knew this was a mess that he needed to help fix. 'We had to sort out a lot of issues with the way things were being done,' he admits, so rather than leave he stayed on another six months.

Over 35 years later Hoenger is still in the industry, as an aviation investigator consulting for insurers. He admits there remain problems with compliance in general aviation. '[CASA, the current regulator] still insist on service manuals, but most people put them on the shelf and never use them . . . Any aviation investigator will tell you that a safe aeroplane is not always legal, and a legally [compliant] plane isn't always safe.'

*

TILLAIR 10 year anniversary Back row (L-R) Paul Mann, Alan Chatfield, Rob Cook, James Hoskins, Shane George, Peter Cook (Rowdy), Michael Lucas, Andrew Ringwood, Peter Stendell. 2nd row (L-R): Peter Quinn, Mike Green, Mark Jerdan, Michael Bosworth, David Kienzle, Gordon Ramsay, Mark Diamond, Maurice Geue, Mark DiRosso, Edward Landy. 3rd row (L-R) Tim McCubbin, Geoff Browne, John Tilley, John Marchant, Barney Milosev, Ian Paige, Mark Morley. Front row (L-R): Stuart Palframan, Hugh Cohen, Neil Ker, Tony Markwell, Sean Raynes, Dean Marshall, George Westmacott

What sets Tilley apart as an employer is the fact that not only were lifelong friendships made, but the pilots and office staff, along with their partners, will go to huge efforts to stay in touch. In 1987 Tilley held a party at Pandamus to celebrate the ten-year anniversary of Tillair's commencement. An astounding 32 ex and current Tillair pilots flew in from around the country to celebrate a man and a business that had given their career and sense of self such an enormous boost.

Since then there have been golf days and other reunions every two or so years around the country, with old staff members flying in from around the globe to attend. Pilots John Torr and Tim McCubbin have been the tireless organisers for many of these.

Of these reunions, Peter Quinn observes: 'The love in the room for Tilley is real. I've had two great mentors: my father is one and Tilley another.' Quinn went on to become CEO of two Qantas subsidiaries, Australian Airlines and Jetconnect. In each workplace he tried to apply the sense of community that he learned from Tilley. 'There's a lot of Tillair in the things I did in life.'

*

Given his addiction to deal making via phone, it was unsurprising that Tilley was an earlier adopter of mobile-phone technology when it emerged in Australia. By 1988, even in Katherine, Tilley could use his 14-kilo analogue car-based phone. It had a 45 cm handset, a receiver in the boot of the car and an antenna on the roof. The $4,000 cost was similar to that of a budget car.

These phones had little memory: they could store just sixteen numbers. The Telecom phone alerted drivers of incoming calls by honking the horn and flashing the headlights. One band frequency needed to be allocated to each call, limiting the number of connections. Tilley recalls: 'I had one big brick. Catching up with the boys after a golf match at a restaurant, I handed it around . . . We're all pissed and everyone was ringing Gundy at Cathay Pacific and all over.'

By the time they were ready to go home the phone had vanished. The theft cost Tilley $4,000.

*

When Hoenger finally confessed to Tilley he wanted out, his friend supported him. Tilley was also tired of the constant problems associated with such a large enterprise, which had become far removed from the family-feel operation Tillair had once been.

Before he left Tilley begged Hoenger to document the business' spare parts inventory, which was still all in Hoenger's head, so Hoenger's first experience with a computer was to input the records of exactly what inventory they held. In mid-1987, after finding a replacement chief engineer, Hoenger finally resigned, taking a role with Hawker Pacific in Cairns. By the time Hoenger left Tillair had bases in Adelaide, Brisbane, Alice Springs, Tennant Creek and Uluru.

Left: The TILLAIR crew still come together every year or two to play golf and reminisce. John Torr; Mike Strong; John Tilley

Above: Tillair/Chartair Golf Day (L-R) Back row: Alan Chatfield, John Marchant, John Torr, Gary Boxall, Peter Quinn, Barney Milosev, Rob Cook, Peter Cook, Richard Duldig, Ross Layther (ATC), Bryce Baud; Middle row: Tim McCubbin, David Jones, Brian Smith, John Tilley, Dave Barclay (ATC), Mark Jerdan, Hugh Cohen; Front: Gordon Ramsay; Mike Cottell; Stuart Palframan; Mike Strong, Keith Tym

Left: Tilley hosted a final Pandamus get together to mark his exit in 1988 (L to R) Mike Cottell; Tracey Norris, Michael Bosworth; Neil Kerr, John Tilley

SELLING UP

Ian Paige recalls a particularly bad day of flying in 1988. 'I was pretty senior at that time. There was a lot going down and we had broken aeroplanes and charters that weren't working.' Paige had to start making operational decisions to address the issues.

'Everybody's not in agreement . . . tempers were rising and everyone was jumping up and down,' Paige recalls. 'John knew things were going badly, he knew it was a mess, and he rang me up. He didn't tell me off; he didn't say do something different. He just says, "Ian, what is it you need me to do? What can I do from here that's going to help you?"'

Tilley could not afford to ignore the mounting risks he bore, running a private operation of the size Tillair had become. He was increasingly concerned. 'If we had a bad accident . . . that would be shocking. If we killed someone or did something . . . Maybe it was time to get out. Take to the blue sky . . . I think part of the trick when you're in business is knowing when to . . . come out of the market.'

The demands of running an airline the size of Tillair were becoming too much. Tilley by then had massive turnover but also a lot of debt, and there was too much stress and not enough enjoyment. The business had many valuable assets, which meant

Australia's top airlines, Air North and Tillair, join forces.

Darwin's AIR NORTH and Katherine's TILLAIR have joined forces to provide the Top End with a bigger, better air service than it's ever had... a service that will meet the growing demand as the Territory develops over the coming years.

Under the AIR NORTH banner, the new airline will service ports all across the Top End... Bathurst Island, Borroloola, Cooinda, Darwin, Elcho Island, Garden Point, Gove, Groote Eylandt, Hooker Creek, Jabiru, Kalkgurung, Ngunkurr, Numbulwar, Oenpelli, Peppiminati, Ramingining, Snake Bay, Tindal, Victoria River and Wave Hill.

And, as well as its comprehensive passenger and freight service AIR NORTH will maintain TILLAIR'S regular mail-run service to Territory stations and settlements.

For Airline Reservations and Freight Enquiries, call
DARWIN: 81 7477 KATHERINE: 72 1711
or your local agent.

For all Air Charter requirements, call
DARWIN: 81 7188; A/hr. 85 4518
KATHERINE: 72 1711; A/hr. 72 1140

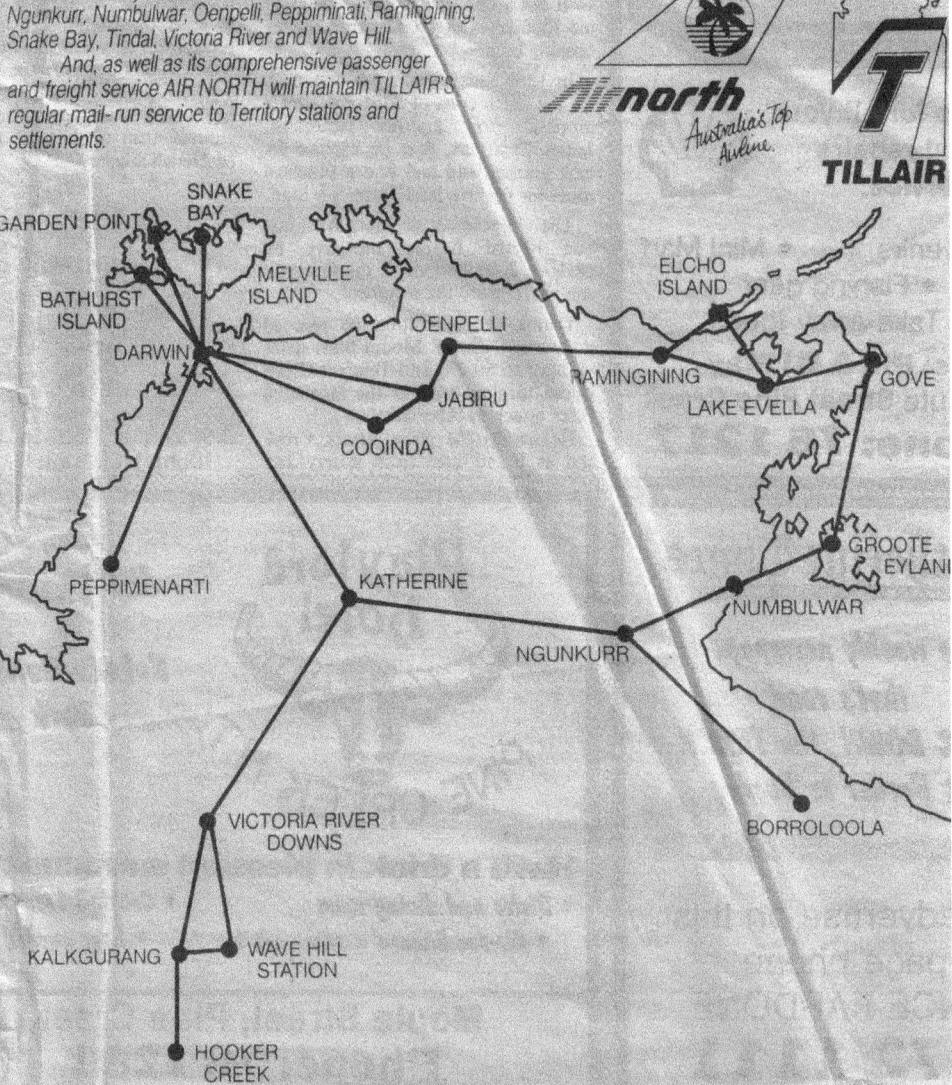

KATHERINE TIMES WEDNESDAY OCTOBER 5

'a fair bit of blue sky'. It might be time to cashing in his business equity.

*

At one stage TNT were considering buying Tillair; however, it came with a condition: John Tilley would need to remain. TNT started negotiations, but Tilley was firm because he had no interest in staying on. 'I'd rather just sell out and take my money,' he said, so in 1988 he sold his Alice Springs air operations – planes, maintenance hangars and routes – to his local opposition, Roger Leach at Skyport. This sale also included the medical work and mail-run routes from Tennant Creek and a scenic flight licence out of Uluru.

In a further multi-million dollar takeover, in September 1988 Airnorth bought all Tillair's Katherine and Top End routes, including around twenty aircraft. An advertisement in the Katherine Times sold the takeover as a merger: 'Australia's top airlines, Airnorth and Tillair, join forces'.

Adelaide-based Rossair, with its Cessna dealership, was also confirmed as joining the group. Tilley announced all Tillair staff would keep their jobs and the Katherine base would retain its identity, yet there was no mention of Tilley leaving. At Pandamus, Tilley hosted a 'wake' for his young charges. It was a glum affair. Tilley is the first to admit that it had been his fifteen years with Elders that had enabled him to build extraordinary bush networks and taught him how to deal with clients and balance his books.

Tilley might have been the rainmaker who won the work, but he remains quick to admit that none of Tillair's success could have been achieved without the extraordinary commitment of his team: pilots, office staff and engineering crew.

*

Without John Tilley there to provide insights into the local customers and their needs the new management struggled. Within a few years, Airnorth on-sold the Katherine-based routes to Roger Leach, giving Leach all the subsidised air-mail routes.

Stuart Palframan was one of many Tillair pilots who grieved when Tilley sold. Palframan stayed on with the new owner Airnorth for a while 'but it just wasn't the same'. Palframan recalls that once he was at Airnorth, Tilley ringing him for one last favour: could he fly Tilley's Cessna 402 VH-ROS down from Katherine to Alice Springs and help him empty the Alice Springs hangar of as many spare parts as they could, then fly all the gear to Adelaide to be stored?

Palframan says, laughing, 'I shouldn't say this, but I think we took a little bit more than we should have . . . I'm sure that half of it wasn't his.'

*

Tilley was approached by his friend at the Cattlemen's Association, John Dyer, who recommended him to assist the Territory government as a consultant, educating farmers on tuberculosis management strategies. Tilley was elected to a plum position on the Northern Territory Pastoral Land Board, and for the first time he became a charter flight customer. The Northern Territory government were paying for him to 'go out to these properties and liaise and convince farmers that they should be joining the program and getting all the blood testing done'.

In his land board role, Tilley's brief was to ensure pastoral properties were keeping up with all their covenants. 'We were converting pastoral leases to perpetual pastoral leases . . . Before they were granted that new title, the land board would fly around and inspect all the properties to make sure they had good cattle yards and fences and water. If they got a tick box, then we'd recommend that they could upgrade their title from 40-year to 99-year leases and make it a perpetual pastoral lease.'

*

Tilley could not ever turn his back on the young pilots he had nurtured to become leaders in commercial aviation, so when the 1989 Australian domestic pilots' dispute caused havoc within the industry, Tilley was on the phone to help broker re-employment deals.

The dispute, co-ordinated by the pilots' union to support its campaign for a 29.5 per cent pay increase, would be one of the most expensive and dramatic in the nation's history. The Australian Federation of Air Pilots (AFAP) had imposed a limitation on the hours they were prepared to work, arguing that if they were to be treated in the same way as other employee groups then their work conditions should also be the same.

> *Tilley could not turn his back on the young pilots he had nurtured, so when the 1989 pilots' dispute caused havoc, he was on the phone to help broker re-employment deals.*

The dispute was superficially resolved after the mass resignation of a significant number of domestic airline pilots to avoid litigation from the airlines. In a strong-arm move from government and airline owners, the pilots' award wage was cancelled and the union deregistered. Seasoned pilots such as Gordon Ramsay reckon the real reason the AFAP was shut down was because they were not a part of the Australian Council of Trade Unions, and thus a threat to the top union body.

While the airlines recruited new pilots from overseas, many ex-Tillair pilots were suddenly without work. Ian Paige was one of these. Back with Ansett again by 2001, Paige was again in trouble when the airline collapsed in the wake of the 9/11 terrorist attacks. 'I had two significant, very complicated periods. I had young triplets at that stage and I had a lot going on, but within 48 hours of both of those events John Tilley was on the phone saying, "Ian, I'm not your boss now, but what can I do? What do you need?"'

Paige ended up immediately getting work through one of Tilley's contacts. 'He had me up and running and paying my bills .. within 48 hours.'

The domestic pilots' dispute had pushed Peter Davies to leave not only Ansett but also the country. He had about ten years as a pilot overseas before returning to join Impulse Airlines, initially flying 100-seater jets. Ultimately, Impulse morphed into Jetstar, and by 2013 Jestar had taken delivery of its first Boeing 787 Dreamliner. Davies was one of the first to fly these. At first, 'They had a lot of problems,' he recalls.

When Qantas first started taking delivery of Dreamliners in 2017, given his experience it was Junior who was training up dozens of Qantas pilots in the huge aircraft, accompanying them in line training. When old colleagues from Tillair such as Gecko George started turning up for Junior to train, despite the jets being so much easier and safer to fly than the Tillair bug smashers they had learned on it was just like old times.

At least five Tillair pilots – Peter Quinn, Keith Tym, Tim McCubbin, Paul Grant and Mike Strong – progressed to captain the world's largest passenger aircraft, Qantas' A380 planes. Many more have an ongoing relationship with their first boss. Mike Cottell sums up what others express: 'There's a bond between us that's hard to describe . . . like an older brother. We all benefited. I may not have been in Qantas the last 30-plus years if it hadn't been for Tilley. I owe him a lot. A lot . . . He's part and parcel of the career I've been able to achieve.'

> **At least five Tillair pilots – Peter Quinn, Keith Tym, Tim McCubbin, Paul Grant and Mike Strong – progressed to captain the world's largest passenger aircraft, Qantas' A380 planes.**

Admits Stuart Palframan, 'Look, I owe everything to John and Brownie. My success and failures in life . . . my experiences, I trace that back, all of it, pretty well back to John and Brownie giving me the job. I just count myself as so lucky. [Getting the job] wasn't through skill or knowledge or anything like that . . . They gave me an opportunity and I could never thank them enough for it.'

*

Tilley could finally slow down and reconnect with his old mates, and he started playing tennis on a Saturday and enjoying life on the farm. Still, farming did not come naturally to him. When daughter Kate returned from boarding school one weekend she noticed their canola crop was not bright yellow like those of all the neighbours. Querying her father, he snapped: 'No, I put the wrong chemical on.'

He has huge self-belief, admits daughter Kate. 'He's never had anyone question him, compare themselves. That freedom is huge.' However, his old frenetic work pace was just around the next bend.

BACK IN THE INDUSTRY

In 1989 the sales of his airline assets allowed Tilley to acquire his dream property in the Burra district of South Australia. Petherton station was an established historic sheep and cropping property. Once a very large holding, like many stations its acreage had been whittled down over recent decades, though it retained its grand homestead. When Tilley walked into the local Burra pub after two decades' absence, he found nothing had changed. His old mates from Elders days welcomed him back as though it had been just two weeks since he had been gone.

Tilley would gaze out over the hills to a neighbouring 700-acre merino stud called Collinsville. Its owners had invested hugely in the stud but had badly mismanaged the business and it went into receivership with its lenders owing $45 million. Tilley had capital still in the bank and had been eyeing off the place for three years, so when the auction came up he pounced.

In around 1994 another nearby property came up for auction in the district, the historic 6,000-acre Willogoleche. Over a century old, pastoralist brothers John and Alfred Hallett had run the station back in the 1860s. Decimated by a drought, they had clawed back from the brink of ruin to rebuild a pastoral empire. The homestead featured wide verandahs, a garden, tennis courts and a wattle park.

Sited on the western side of Hallett, the homestead was about two miles from the town. Tilley could not resist: selling the King Air 200 he had been leasing out gave him the funds for the purchase.

*

The mining boom accelerated demand for aircraft and Tilley was there to fulfil the need. In the mid-1990s he bought into an aircraft brokership called Aeromil with Steve Padgett. Lenders would repossess planes where their owners had defaulted and Aeromil would step in to find a new owner. It was this Aeromil relationship that propelled Tilley into purchasing and leasing aircraft. Steve Padgett suggested to Tilley the first deal involving a King Air, and to Tilley the opportunity was attractive. If he bought a plane for a good price and located a lessee who would guarantee to fly the aircraft for a minimum number of hours per week, as an income-producing asset he could borrow almost 100 per cent of the value. The leasing income would pay the loan mortgage and more.

> **The mining boom accelerated demand and Tilley was there to fulfil the need. In the mid-1990s he bought into an aircraft brokership called Aeromil.**

Aircraft do not devalue significantly so they can be sold for almost as much as they were purchased for. For his first client, Tilley quickly found a lessee for the King Air. The Adelaide-based National Jet Company had just won a contract to fly miners in and out of Cairns to the Ok Tedi copper and gold mines in New Guinea. Within months Tilley fell into the business of buying up aircraft cheaply when lenders had repossessed them. Effectively an aircraft banker, he started leasing these planes out to airlines that needed them. Later, he took advantage of a US recession to buy up aircraft there.

Says Mark Jerdan: 'Tilley knows exactly what planes are worth, given his time in the industry: how many hours it's flown, how much time left on the propeller. He has the contacts to call the right people to get more information about a plane.'

Tilley admits that given its much smaller population 'Australia is a bit like a third-world country. We always buy the old second-hand stuff that America is finished with and I lease them.' By then Tilley was buying multiple nineteen-seat Bandeirante aircraft. He was adept at spotting a bargain: at times he would purchase an aircraft at a large discount that its lenders had repossessed.

One of Tilley's Bandeirantes went to Darwin and a few to a small commuter airline in New Zealand - a subsidiary of Ansett. Another was leased to work in the Cook Islands and several to Air Fiji, who used them for short passenger flights. When Air Fiji needed a larger 30-seat aircraft but were unable to afford the capital outlay, Tilley stepped in. For the first time he purchased a 30-seat Brasilia from Flight West, leasing it to Air Fiji to fly passengers from Fiji to Tuvalu and Tonga.

Air Fiji ultimately ran into financial trouble, squeezed out by Fiji Airlines. Air Fiji was one of several customers who defaulted on Tilley's monthly lease repayments. 'I had to find another lessee. I walked out of there with my fingers burned,' Tilley admits of the Air Fiji relationship, 'but one cannot hold on to these setbacks. I always focus on moving forward.'

In later years Flight West came back to Tilley: this time they wanted Tilley to lease them a Brasilia.

*

Tilley is 'one of the few people in general aviation [who] actually makes any money!' admits Tim McCubbin. Over his career John Tilley has bought or leased well over 100 aircraft, not just from the US but also from the most unlikely of countries including Uganda, Costa Rica, Russia and Puerto Rico.

Before video technology was so good, Tilley would always travel to inspect the planes. 'But now . . . I just get them to do a video and I look at it. Show me this. Take this piece, take this cowl off and show me here and this wing fitting. Show me inside it. Show me the hood liner.' There are now just six leased aircraft on Tilley's roster, including three Brasilias. He learned to keep track of his fleet via a satellite feed to his

> **Over his career John has bought or leased well over 100 aircraft, not just from the US but also from the most unlikely of countries including Uganda and Puerto Rico**

mobile phone, telling him where the aircraft are, their flight plans and whether they are being handled correctly.

*

Tilley had divorced Jenny in 1988. Come 1997 on a Friday night prior to the Adelaide Crows first Grand Final, a woman called Suzy Burford walked into John's life. Suzy was totally different from John, yet their initial dating quickly become serious. Suzy quickly dubbed her new beau 'Tilley' -soon no-one – neither friends nor family – called him John.

In January 2000 Suzy and Tilley married. Suzy was finally able to push Tilley out of his comfort zone, encouraging him to take holidays and time out to spend time with family and friends.

When the Twin Towers were brought down in New York on 11 September 2001, Tilley and Suzy were on holidays at Lake Como. Within days and amid the global panic, airlines everywhere had to change how they operated. Ansett, already in financial trouble, struggled with the new security requirements, and for smaller players such as Flight West they could ill afford the new security measures. They collapsed, leaving Tilley with an unleased aircraft. In this business, cash flow was crucial and suddenly Tilley's had stalled.

At the time Perth-based Lindsay Evans had a 30-seat Brasilia he was operating for a mining company. The young pilot was short a second aircraft, so Tilley lost no time in getting on the phone from Europe: he had a plane sitting in Brisbane earning nothing. 'Take it to Perth,' he said to Lindsay. 'Just pay me for the hours you do.'

Lindsay's company went on to become a key leasing client of Tilleys, providing 30-seater Brasilia FIFO services to the booming mining industry. At one stage Tilley and Evans flew together to the

CESSNA
CARAVAN I

An outstanding aircraft in as new condition

Only 1200 hrs. approx. total time with recent HSI.

Immaculate presentation and available immediately.

Priced significantly below cost of equivalent new aircraft.

If not sold within a few weeks, market demand will necessitate flying this highly successful aircraft overseas.

Currently on the Australian register, so don't let this popular and valuable aircraft leave the country. It will be impossible to replace.

An excellent investment.

For price and full details, please contact Steve Padgett.

AEROMIL

Aeromil Australia Pty Ltd
277 King Street, Mascot NSW 2020
Telephone (02) 667 3881
Fax (02) 693 5951

US to look at SkyWest's fleet of Brasilia aircraft. SkyWest was the biggest Brasilia fleet operator in America. Advised to go to an airport in Little Arkansas, they were greeted by 45 second-hand planes lined up on the tarmac: all had been traded in for regional jets.

Evans and Tilley each bought one, engaging a ferry pilot as Tilley had done many times before to fly the aircraft to Australia. These guys had a specialised role in flying small planes across the Pacific to their buyers. David Friend was Tilley's ferry pilot in those days. Given the purchased planes were designed for far shorter legs, Friend needed to connect up an extra fuel tank. Much of the payload was fuel, allowing him to fly from California to Honolulu in one hop. From there he would head down to Pago Pago in American Samoa, overnight and refuel and head straight for the Gold Coast. In more recent times Tom Lopes from Gateway Aviation has flown out his Caravan purchases in the same manner. Tilley swears the $50,000 charged by these ferry pilots was well worth the cost.

Meanwhile, Lindsay's Network Aviation grew to the point where Lindsay was able to buy aircraft of his own, and he ended up with seven in his fleet. It was so successful that Qantas eventually made an offer to buy that Lindsay could not refuse. Seeing his protégés have such success gave Tilley immense satisfaction.

In the mid-2000s Tilley's Brasilias were sold into South Africa. 'They had 40,000 airframe hours on them and I'm sure they'll still be flying with another 20,000 hours over there!' jokes Tilley.

*

One day at Cairns airport Tilley noticed a fourteen-seater Cessna Caravan on the tarmac. He learned its owners had been unable to pay the GST owing and that it had sat in limbo at the Cairns base for the past twelve months. Tilley had one of those back in the early 1980s around Alice Springs. He rang up and bought it, then he had to find it a home.

Brent Hanson was a Broome pilot Tilley knew; his Broome Aviation business was leasing Cessna 210s. Tilley encouraged him to lease the larger Cessna Caravan as well. Later, Hanson won the contact for the FIFO work for Mount Gibson Iron, and brought its workers back and forth from Broome to Koolan Island. It meant Tilley was able to lease Brent further planes.

Tilley was proud of the leg up he gave to these young pilots to help them grow until they had the capital to purchase planes themselves. 'People always ring me if they want a Caravan. [These days] I don't advertise.'

*

Tilley returned to property purchases - building up extensive landholdings in the lower part of South Australia. The first property he purchased was the 5,000-acre Moonee Hills station south of Meningie, down the bottom of Lake Albert and close to Coorong National Park. His purchases in this district expanded: Moonee Hills South, Marshes, Alamil, Yalanda, The Needles, Stoneywell and finally Shoreditch.

For a time Tilley and Suzy lived in a cottage accommodation at Moonee Hills. In 2016 Tilley made another major change - selling his much-loved Petherton. In doing so, he farewelled a wonderful old horse Delhi - with him since his early days at Pandamus.

All their antique furniture was transferred to Alamil which became their new go-to country residence.

*

Tilley's daughter Kate, who now works closely with her father, recognises how he operates. In 2010 she started sitting with her father one day a week doing his IT. The role slowly grew, keeping her father afloat in the modern world.

'He has a photographic memory for details but we both hate contracts and reading the fine details. When dealing with Dad his word is his honour; the paperwork is just a formality. If he agrees to someone over the phone he'll honour it! He works on gut instinct.'

Kate notes that in the last two decades her father would not have continued to achieve what he has without assistance. 'The world has moved so quickly over the last fifteen years, but who needs to do the little things when you are dealing with the big picture and working on deals that blow my mind all the time? It's not uncommon for Dad to run through the pros and cons of each plane he has his eye on and the digging he has done to uncover anything not listed on the online listing. We love to use geotags to work out dates photos are taken and search for photos to see if the plane has been in a hanger or left on the tarmac.

'I never know what the day will bring. Only last week Dad called to ask me to drive to Adelaide airport to pick up Cessna Caravan seats then drive them four hours to Naracoorte to meet a young pilot. At the airport we swapped out the seats, reloaded and dropped them back to Adelaide. It was a fourteen-hour road trip but I love to be able to help out.'

*

Over the years Tilley's blended family has grown through much loved grandchildren the first - Erin, Sam, and Lara- were followed years later by what Tilley refers to as a "second drop" - Grace,

Maddy, Olivia, Lily, Baxter, Sienna, Eliza, and Harry. Already there are three great grandchildren and one more on the way.

Scott Tilley had spent much of his working life as a chartered accountant in public practice, feeling bad that he hadn't come back to work in the family business with his father as had been the original plan when he left school, even though he had acted as an accountant for his father since 1987. In 2016 Scott Tilley started to say, 'I'm probably ready to come in . . . The bit that appealed to me the most was the aviation side because I'd grown up with planes with Dad.'

Scott was surprised when Tilley could not remember the conversation from 37 years earlier. His dad admitted: 'You've been working with me all this time. We've been helping each other, but I'm not planning to hand anything over. I am still the man in charge.' A year later Tilley told his son: 'There's this young guy I know in Sydney . . . he wants to get into aircraft leasing. I'm gonna help him, mentor him.'

Scott exploded. 'What the hell? What about me? I wanted to do that!' Scott ultimately got into aircraft leasing, though on his own rather than as part of the family business. Nonetheless, his father tracked down an Australian-built Gipps Aero Airvan that needed a new engine.

'Okay, Scott, you're going to buy that,' Tilley advised. To Scott this was a surprise: his father had always been a Cessna man. Only a few months earlier he had canned the idea of an Airvan when Scott raised it with him.

> **Everyone who knows Dad knows that most of the best ideas come from him**

'Everyone who knows Dad knows that most of the best ideas come from him,' Scott admits. Ultimately, this was a good way to enter the leasing space. 'We got a time extension on the engine life and earned some revenue to help fund the new one.' Tilley even lent Scott the money to buy this first aircraft and declined to mentor the young Sydney guy.

As well as his own business, Scott also helps his father with business planning but confesses: 'Dad is still the man.' The pair now talk about the aviation industry and new places and opportunities they both see and how to make sure it's a good deal and that the contracts are right. 'He's helped all of us immensely,' Scott admits, 'in his own way. He really does love helping others to start and grow their business.'

In 2019, along with the regular golf day re-union, John Torr organised a surprise 80th birthday party for Tilley. Enlisting the help of daughter Kate, Torr arranged to hire a hangar at Adelaide airport for the event . Tilley was told there would be the standard pub meal at the local pub. 'But first' said Torr, 'you need to check out a Cessna 210 plane I'm looking at out at the airport before we go to dinner' . 'What's the rego? the ever-inquisitive Tilley questioned . "Ah it's just been imported from offshore' Torr lied. The party drew over eighty colleagues and their partners, along with some memorable speeches.

Tilley shouted his own family birthday in the Maldives the same year – the entire

John Tilley's surprise 80th birthday in an Adelaide hangar brought together many friends and family

cohort of 25 children, step-children and grandchildren celebrated for a glorious seven days.

Tilley and Suzy continue to travel widely – initial overseas driving trips with Tilley doing all the driving. 'We had a chauffeur-driven car – me' he would explain to friends. In more recent years, the pair have been enjoying the comfort of cruise-ships. Given Suzy has the wonderful ability to bring people together wherever they venture, the pair have collected many friends who have remained in their lives. Twenty-seven years on, they continue to enjoy time together abroad and in South Australia.

Daughter Penny is working within the agri side of the business, so Tilley talks cattle deals and farming with her all the time. Recently he rang his daughter with the idea that had made him enough to buy his first plane. 'We could buy a mob, skinny and hungry, fatten them up and go halves.' She declined his offer.

While not in her dad's business, Kate still goes into the Adelaide office to help out, clean up the paperwork and sort out computer issues. These days Kate's focus is a piece of land in the Coorong where she has KipPods and an art residency program. 'I hope to be loving what I do for as long as Dad,' she admits.

Tilley's eldest daughter Sarah was the only one to start a business her father knew nothing about – interior design – and raise a family in Sydney. It was her link with me and the passion to tell her father's story that brought this book to fruition.

And Tilley? At 85, he insists on going to work each day, doing what he loves best: mentoring the younger generation, not to mention buying, selling and leasing aircraft.

EPILOGUE

John Tilley was perhaps above all, a mentor. In the decades after they left his employ, Tilley has had a rare talent for keeping in radio contact with the pilots, engineers and admin team he nurtured; celebrating their achievements, attending their weddings, funerals and helping out in crises. He took great pride in observing and sometimes facilitating his employees' career progression and achievements in both domestic and international settings. He even advised some in purchasing aircraft. The Tillair/ChartAir team's close camaraderie, with its roots in the Territory, lives on through an active Facebook group, regular golf days and now this written record of a unique era in outback aviation. The below entries provide a window into the later careers and achievements of many who found their legs in the Territory.

Phil Anderson (Shadow) left Tillair in 1985. He stayed in the region, flying Partenavias for a few months for Maningrida Progress Association, before working for Helimuster. at VRD for two years flying Cessna 182/RG 206s, PA32 Barons and Aerocommander 500s. In 1988, he moved to Lloyd Aviation (which became SkyWest), becoming a First Officer on Bandeirantes and Dash 8s. He went on to captain Banderiantes & King Airs, with stints in Darwin, Cairns and PNG. He and Charmaine married in 1992. In 1995 he spent 18 years with National Jet Systems in Darwin and later Perth as a First Officer on Dash 8s and BAE 146s. He was promoted to captain and

Head of Training and Checking on the Dash 8. In 2018, Phil spent two years captaining Dash 8s for Maroomba Airlines out of Perth. He and Charmaine live in Perth with their three sons.

Shirley Avis left Tillair in 1988, moving to Brisbane, into a role as Night Ops Controller with Norfolk Airlines. A year later, she moved to Cairns with Sunbird Airlines until its closure in 1990. But the Territory called her home. She settled in Darwin, working with Executive Air Charter and National Jet, where she met the father of her two children. Life took a turn, and Shirley embraced the challenges of single motherhood on the Sunshine Coast. Undeterred, Shirley headed to Norfolk Island to work with the South Pacific Hotel Group. Later, Shirley studied counselling and social work. Now, she runs a successful practice helping individuals and couples navigate life's challenges. Her story is one of courage, reinvention and a fierce determination to thrive.

Geoff Browne (Brownie) could not be interviewed for this book, given his death from cancer in 2010. However Brownie played a crucial and pivotal role in the success of Tillair. With a deep love of the outback, he was an encyclopedia of practical and local knowledge regarding both the company's Cessna fleet and the station owners they serviced. He wore multiple hats to his young charges - part mentor, part disciplinarian, part trainer and part customer services manager. After 1989, Brownie remained in Katherine to fly for Lloyds Helicopters who had the search and rescue contract for the RAAF base. When they were bought out by CHC, Brownie stayed on, a vital part of the Katherine community. Following his retirement he and Sue embarked on an extended caravan journey around the country, staying with old friends. Some months into his retirement, Brownie was diagnosed with cancer. Typically, he put family first, purchasing a Perth home for Sue, his daughter Alex and sons Richard and David. When he passed away at the age of 59, Geoff was buried along with a model of his beloved American 1930's Stearman biplane.

Scott Builder left Tillair in May 1988 and joined Hazelton Airlines in Cudal NSW shortly before joining Qantas International in October of that year. At Qantas Scott has flown B747s, B744s, B767s, A330s and is now an A380 Captain based in Sydney. He married Anna in 1993 and has two adult children. His son Jack has been accepted into Qantas 2025 Pilot program. After commuting from Sydney to Alice Springs for over 30 years, the couple recently moved to Robe, South Australia.

Alan Chatfield (Chatty) left Tillair in 1987 to take up a job with Air Niugini flying a Fokker F28. In 2000 he moved onto a Boeing 717 for Impulse Airlines based out of Sydney. Alan went on to fly the A320 for Jetstar until his retirement in 2006. In 1997 he remarried and now lives in Murwillumbah NSW.

Hugh Cohen (Who Coon) left TillAir in 1987, moving to Melbourne to join Pelair. Seven years later he joined Independent Air Freight flying DC9s. From there he moved to Visy flying the GIV and Global Express. Hugh flew his last flight in 2018 after working years as a Flight Officer with Virgin Airlines. He has retired on the Murray River in Southern NSW.

Peter Cook (Rowdy) gained his nicknamed due to his extremely quite persona. Whilst at Tillair he commenced on a Cessna 210 rising up to achieve a command position on a Cessna Conquest prior to leaving for Qantas in 1985. At Qantas Rowdy chose the Boeing 747 as his choice of aircraft, eventually gaining a command prior to leaving Qantas in 2007 having being diagnosed with cancer. Rowdy was just 46 when he passed away in 2008 leaving behind two children, Kate and TJ. TJ chose to follow his father's profession and was endorsed on the Boeing 747 prior to also flying with Qantas.

Michael Cottell (Mick) was one of Tillair's last pilots – his last C210 run from Hooker Creek was logged 31 October 1988. Little more than six weeks later he moved to Sydney, flying B747s for Qantas as a Second Officer. Four years on, he was promoted to First Officer on the B767 and then B744. He married Jacinta in 1995, commuting from Brisbane to Sydney. By early 2002 he was in command of a Qantas B767, later becoming a Check & Training Captain and eventually transferring to the A330 and the B787. He completed a Bachelor of Science (Biological Sciences) and Master of Astronomy during this time. He was based out of Brisbane from 2014. Mike retired in late 2019 – after almost 31 years and 20,000 flying hours with the national carrier.

Pete Davies (Junior) left Tillair in 1988 to join Ansett. When the pilots dispute struck, Pete spent the next decade overseas, flying

Fokker aircraft for Aer Lingus, then Pelangi Air (Malaysia), Royal Brunei (where he met his wife) and the Gill Airways in Finland. He returned to Australia in 2000 to join regional and low-cost operator Impulse which was acquired by Qantas in 2001, absorbing it into Qantaslink. Moving sideways to Jetstar, Peter has been a Check and Training captain on all their aircraft - B717, A320, A330 & currently B787s -over 24 years. Approaching retirement, he lives in Sydney's Newport.

Mark Diamond (Diamo) left Tillair in 1989 taking a role flying a Twin Otter with SkyWest Aviation in Kununurra. A year later he went to Ansett, flying the F28 out of Perth. He married Ansett flight attendant Jackie in 1995 and stayed with the carrier until its demise in 2002. Mark, his wife and two daughters then moved to the USA for five years where Mark worked in construction. Returning to Melbourne in 2007, he took up with Jetstar, becoming an A320/1 captain. He was promoted to Check Captain at Jetstar in 2012. In 2015 Mark took up with China Southern Airlines flying international routes for five years as an A330 Captain, commuting from Los Angeles. After a two year Covid hiatus, Mark has been flying the A330 since 2022 with National Airlines. Now a dual US/ Australian citizen he remains in Los Angeles with his wife of thirty years.

Rosemary Ey departed Katherine in 1982 for husband Terry to further his police career. Regular promotions meant that command positions ensued throughout the Territory. This also provided Rosemary with opportunities to fill senior positions, one being the Chief Minister's representative for the Tennant Creek Region. They left the Territory in 2001 to retire to their family property and vineyard at Coonawarra, South Australia. Terry was police superintendent of the Territory's first and last Cannonball Run in 1994 - a motorsport's race from Darwin to the Rock and back designed to put the Territory on the global stage, but which ended in tragedy.

Shayne George (Gecko) joined Tillair in 1984 and stayed on with the Brisbane based Transair after the sale in 1988. In April 1989 he joined Qantas as a Boeing B747-200/300 Second Officer. In 1995, he was promoted to First Officer flying Boeing B767s. In 2001, he completed further training allowing him to captain B767s for a further 12 years, ten of those as a trainer and examiner. With the retirement of the Qantas B767 in 2014, Shayne transferred to

Captain the fleet's A330. After more than three long years (not an Airbus fan), Shayne returned to captaining the B787 upon its introduction into the Qantas fleet in 2017. With thirty five years under his belt with Qantas, Shayne continues to fly as a B787 Captain and Type Rated Examiner, based in Sydney.

Milly Goodings left Tillair in 1986 to take up a job as Finance and Office Manager with Dick David Fuel Supplies/Road Trains of Australia. Two years later she left to start a family and worked part time for Tilley, doing his personal book-keeping. Not long after, Milly and her husband Brad bought two video stores. Milly ran the retail businesses and was integral in setting up Katherine's first music store and merging the two video stores. Next came a Mitre 10 store. Milly left the businesses and Katherine in 1995 when her marriage ended. She moved to the Gold Coast with her young children as a sole parent with tougher work prospects. After working in various jobs, she secured a position with Riviera Marine in Feb 2000 in their Finance Dept. and worked there for 12 years before being made redundant. Fifteen months later she returned to Riviera where she has remained for the last 11 years and is currently the Wholesale Finance and Administration Manager.

After leaving Tillair, **Ron Hoenger** (Ronbo) (ML)departed Alice Springs to accept a role as Chief Engineer at Hawker Pacific Cairns until July 1988. He moved to Perth in Sep 1988 to take a role as C441 engineer with Barrack Mines. When Barrack Mines folded a few years later, the aviation division was absorbed into Skippers Transport group where Ron remained as Chief Engineer until Aug 1998, when a CASA witch-hunt led Ron to lose his job, his engineering licence and a lot of money. In April 1999, Skippers reemployed Hoenger as a full time C441 pilot, until a medical episode in 2002 meant he was deployed as a Performance Analyst. He spent three years as manager of Aeronautical Engineers Australia, before setting up a Performance Division with Skywest Airlines. Since leaving Skywest in 2010, Hoenger has run a successful aircraft weighing, consulting and aviation insurance assessment business from Perth.

Mark Jerdan (Jerdo) started with Tillair in 1979. His first term ended in 1981 where he went to fly for Broken Hill Air Charter. Marrying Clare in 1982, he returned to Tillair in 1984, earning a

Check and Training Approval rating as well as the ability to renew Instrument ratings. In 1986 he shifted to Darwin (followed by Cairns and Brisbane) to fly Shorts 330 and Israeli Westwind 1124 for Pelair. In 1988, he accepted a job offer at Qantas. Here he flew the Boeing 747 200, the 747 300, B747 SP, 767s, 747-400s, B737s and B787-9. He became a Captain in 2005. For the three years 2015-2018, he took leave without pay from Qantas to fly Boeing 787 for Qatar Airways based in Doha. Returning to Qantas, he flew with them until his retirement to Byron Bay in 2020.

In 1988, **Ian Lucas** left Uluru for Brisbane - unemployed with over 5,000 flying hours. He flew Bandierantes and Dash 8's for Sunstate Airlines until 2001. By then he was remarried to Lee and had twins, Sam and Meg. He flew B717's and A320s for Impulse Airlines (which morphed into Qantaslink then Jetstar) before tiring of the low-cost airline life. Ian left the industry permanently in 2007 having flown about 17,500 hours. Since then, Ian spend a decade building a successful accommodation and concert venue business - Lucas Parklands - surrounded by tropical rainforest in Montville, Queensland. Pre- aviation Ian had been an accomplished pianist and Lee encouraged him to return to the keyboard. He practiced daily. Although his fingers, arms and back ached, Ian rediscovered his passion. Twice he has won a national competition for the best amateur pianist aged over 30. Lucas Parklands continues to provide performance opportunities for young musicians.

Mike Lucas (ML) married Tillair reservations clerk Joan Petersen in 1985. He left Tillair in 1987 after being accepted into Ansett, initially flying the F27 and F50 in Sydney, then moving onto the B737 based in Melbourne. The pilots dispute in August 1989 meant a resignation from Ansett and short stint in General Aviation before moving to Kuala Lumpur to fly the B737 and A300 for Malaysia Airlines. Mike returned to Australia in 1994 to take up a position with National Jet Systems on the BAe146 and Avro RJ70, including various check and training roles. He was variously based in Brisbane, Cairns, Darwin and Adelaide before settling in Perth. Mike joined Virgin in early 2001, flying the B737 and holding various check and training positions from bases in Brisbane and Melbourne. Mike retired in mid 2019 and now lives in regional Victoria.

John Marchant (Marcho) joined Tillair in late 1977, having commenced an aircraft engineer apprenticeship with Qantas. But John liked the idea of flying aircraft more than fixing them. He was one of Tillair's earliest pilots who went on to become Chief Pilot. He flew every aircraft type that Tilley acquired, including the C-550 (Citation II). His skills were never wasted. Many a time he was to be found fixing aircraft. Every Tillair pilot knew John Marchant. After Tillair, John flew out of Perth for a year before going to Melbourne to fly Westwinds for Pelair. Then he joined Ansett, staying around a decade, captaining B-737s. John passed away peacefully on his farm in August 2023, leaving behind his lifelong partner Shelley, daughter Joedy, son Matthew and three loving grandchildren.

Tim McCubbin (Muckabin) left Tillair in November 1985 to take up with Qantas as a Second Officer on the 747. He was promoted to First Officer on the 767 in October 1988, two weeks after marrying Jenny who he had met in Katherine, where she worked for the School of the Air. Tim was promoted to Captain Qantas 767s exactly ten years to the day after joining the national carrier and continued to fly the 767 until August 2006 when he moved to the 747-400 and then to the A380 in March 2012. He was a Check & Training Captain on both the 767 and the 744. Tim retired in December 2020 and lives in Brisbane where he plays as much golf as possible and spends time with his children Jessica, Rhiannon and Taylor and his three (soon to be four) grandchildren.

Barney Milosevic moved from Tillair's Brisbane base to Australian Airlines in September 1986 to train as First Officer on the Jetstream J31. The next year he built a house, sold it and divorced. When the J31 operations ceased in early 1988 Barney was dispatched to Melbourne to train on the Douglas DC9. Halfway in, this was also cancelled. In mid 1988 he relocated to Townsville as FO on DHC6 Twin Otter. Then it was back to Melbourne to train as FO on Boeing B737-300. A day before endorsement the Pilots Dispute started, forcing Barney back to General Aviation. Back in Perth, Barney flew a C441 Conquest for CorpAir and Barrack Mines. In February 1990 he returned to Australian Airlines flying B737s from Melbourne. Barney moved to Woodend to live the country lifestyle and breed cattle. Meeting flight attendant Jelica in 1992, they married the next year. Australian Airlines merged with QANTAS and by 1995 Barney was in command on its B737s. In 1998 the family moved to

Gisborne a bit closer to Melbourne, expanding to include two girls and a son. In 2014 Barney bought a Cessna 177RG Cardinal which he hires out as a side hustle. He continues to fly B737-800s (maxing his hours every month), having now clocked up over 34,000 flying hours. Barney and Jelica have been married nearly 32 years.

Ken Norman (Ken Cool) left Tillair in 1983 to complete year 12 level Maths, Physics and English in Adelaide, given this was a prerequisite for employment in a commercial airline. The same year he married Cathyrn Orla. Initially Ken worked as flying instructor at Parafield in Adelaide. In 1988 he joined Tilley's old partner Erno Sopru, flying Air Charter Cessna 310's and 402's from Adelaide. In 1989 he joined Ansett flying Fokker 50s as Flight Officer. After the 1989 pilots dispute he flew De Havilland Doves, Cessna, Piper, Beechcraft and Aero Commanders out of Essendon. In 1994, Norman joined John Torr's Jet City flying medical retrieval and organ transplant flights. In 1997, he joined Crown Melbourne bringing in high rollers worldwide on Gulfstream G-IV and G-V's. In 2012, he took on a role as rich-lister Paul Little's private pilot flying Gulfstreams worldwide. Ken continues to fly both G650 and DC3 aircraft professionally out of Melbourne.

When **Ian Paige** (Paigey) left Tillair in November 1986 he moved to Melbourne, flying F27s. F50s and B737's as First Officer for Ansett. That ended in August 1989 due to the pilots dispute. Like many, Ian looked offshore, moving to Kuala Lumpur to join Malaysia Airlines as First officer flying B737s and the A300. He returned to Melbourne and Ansett in May 1992, flying the A320, before relocating with Ansett to Cairns in 1996 as a BAe146 Captain. When Ansett wound up In September 2001, he had six months off before joining Virgin in Brisbane, as training captain on the B737. Seven year later he was promoted to line captain B737-300 and remained in this role for ten years until his retirement in February 2019. Ian and Leanne live in Brisbane and raised four children.

When Tillair was sold to Air North in 1989 **Stuart Palframan** stayed on for a year, then joined Ansett, at first flying Fokker 28s. He remained with Ansett until its collapse in September 2001. After that, he flew for Eva Air out of Taipei, then moved to Hong Kong to fly for Oasis. Roles with Jetstar (initially from Auckland then based out of Sydney) were followed by a secondment to introduce the

A320 to Network Aviation (Qantaslink) out of Perth, then back to Jetstar in Sydney. Still in Sydney, he is currently on a secondment to introduce the A220 to National Jet Systems (Qantaslink). Since leaving TillAir Stuart has earned ratings to fly the FK28, B747, B747-400, A320/A321, B717 and the BD500 (A220). As well as various management roles, Stuart has earned credentials as a Flight Examiner, Flight Instructor as well as a Check and training pilot.

After two tours **Peter Quinn** (Quinny) left Tillair to join Qantas in 1980. A couple of years later he took a leave of absence from Qantas, returning to Tillair for a third time. During this time he met and married Sue then returned to Qantas. At Qantas Peter flew the HS125, 747 variants, the 767, and the Airbus A 380. In addition, he spent time in training management and as Chief Pilot at Australian Airlines before becoming CEO. Following the closure of Australian Airlines, Peter became CEO of Jetconnect in New Zealand. Following COVID, retirement beckoned. However a few years of retirement was all Peter could bear. In 2024 he returned to the workforce in a fulltime management role with Virgin Australia in Brisbane.

Gordon Ramsay (Gundy) left Tillair in late 1985 to take up a job with Trans Australia Airlines (TAA) in Melbourne on the DC-9 and 737. Within 3 years he had moved on to Cathay Pacific in Hong Kong where he flew for 33 years, flying worldwide on the Boeing 747- 200/300/400, Airbus A330/340/340-600 and Boeing 777-200/300/300ER. He married Lita in 1984. He retired to the NSW Northern Rivers in 2022, buying a Diamond DA62 light twin plane and still flies for fun.

Mike Strong (Dangles) left Tillair in 1984 to take up a job with Qantas where he remained for 36 years. Mike initially flew B747s as Second officer & First Officer. Six years on he captained 767 and went on to captain the 747, 744 and A380. Mike also held the positions of Senior Check Captain (TRE) 744 & 744 and Check & Training Captain A380. He retired in 2020 during the COVID A380 fleet grounding with a redundancy offer). He now lives on the Gold Coast.

John Torr (JT) left Chartair in August 1986 to join TAA based out of Longreach flying a Cessna 310 for the Flying Surgeon Service. In 1988 he moved to Melbourne, training on Australian Airlines DC9 as Copilot. Like scores of pilots during the 1989 pilot dispute, JT was pressured to resign. But with a Cessna Citation endorsement he remained in demand. He started as a corporate jet captain on a Cessna Citation. Then he and another pilot founded JetCity, a private and commercial Charter/Management operation. When one of their aircraft leasors filed for bankruptcy, JT borrowed and mortgaged his home to purchase the Citation, quickly flipping it for a Learjet he used for Medivac flights to Australians injured overseas. In early 1995 JT met Lloyd Williams who soon employed him as his personal pilot. When Williams was awarded the Crown Casino contract, a Gulfstream GIV was acquired to bring in High Level patrons. Soon JT was flying Kerry and James Packer and assisting in the flight crew operations of the Packer's Bombardier Global Express. JT's Territory experience changed the Australian corporate aviation scene as he endorsed Copilots and trained them in all facets: dealing with entertainment and sports celebrities; how to arrange customs and quarantine for international operations; International landing and overflight permits as well as booking accommodation, food and beverage for Guests. It was Tillair on a much larger scale. The Crown operations eventually operated with multiple Gulfstream GIV's then GV's and eventually Bombardier Global Express aircraft. Forced to step away in 2006 due to a medical condition, he returned to Jet City in 2008. By the time he sold in 2009, JetCity had owned a Piper Navajo, a Beechcraft Baron a Citation, a Learjet 24 and multiple Learjet 35 and 36 series jets. In 2010 JT flew a Bombardier Express for a Melbourne family, operate at heights up to 50,000 feet at speeds up to Mach .90 he flew into places as varied as Russia, Africa, Aspen, St Moritz and New York. He enjoyed camel polo in Mongolia, a live volcano erupting in Cuba and driving Huskies through the Finland forests. With the onset of Covid in 2020, after 45 years and 17,500 flying hours, JT retired from aviation.

Tim Travers-Jones left Tillair in 1989, taking a role flying Chieftains with Hazelton Airlines. After a few years, he moved to Brisbane to take up as a Flight Officer with Australian Airlines, flying 737s until its merger with Qantas in 1993. He rose to command 737s. Tim married in 1992, lives on the Sunshine Coast, and is currently a check and training captain on Qantas 787s. His proudest achievement has been his happy marriage and four children. His oldest son David also became a pilot and is now a 787 Second Officer with Qantas.

Keith Tym left Tillair early in 1984 when Qantas offered him a job flying Boeing 747s internationally. He married in 1985 and through work was able to travel extensively. Keith went on to fly the new Qantas 747-400, then 767s (internationally and domestically), back to the 747 and finally eleven years flying A380s including five as a Check and Training Captain. Covid triggered a premature retirement in 2020. But he was not done. In 2022 Keith moved from Sydney to Adelaide and in 2024, forty years on, the wheel turned full circle. He is now flying Tilley around in his new toy - a TBM 700. Keith and Muin have four adult children.

TILLAIR-CHARTAIR STAFF 1977 - 1988

TILLAIR-CHARTAIR STAFF 1977 - 1988

(Note surnames at time of employment are used)

FIRST NAME	SURNAME	ROLE
Gary	Allen	Alice Springs Maintenance
Phil	Anderson (Shadow)	Pilot
Paul	Ballard	Pilot
Colin	Barge	Engineer Apprentice
Dean	Barrett	Alice Springs Maintenance
Bryce	Baud (Bad)	Chartair Operations Manager
Kate	Best	Katherine Office
Mike	Bosworth (Bossy)	Pilot
Simon	Boulton	Alice Springs Maintenance
Gary	Boxall (Box)	Pilot
Anne	Brooksbank	Alice Springs Office
Melanie	Brown	Katherine Office
Geoff	Browne (Brownie)	Pilot
Jeff	Buchanan	Pilot
Scott	Builder	Pilot
Dennis	Caddies	Alice Springs Maintenance
Allan	Chatfield (Chatty)	Pilot
Julianne	Coe	Yulara Office
Hugh	Cohen (Who Coon)	Pilot
Steve	Coleman	Alice Springs Office
Deborah	Coleman	Katherine Office
Grant	Colman	Pilot
Peter	Cook (Rowdy)	Pilot
Rob	Cooke (Cookie Monster)	Pilot
Richard	Cornish	Pilot
Murray	Cosson	Pilot
Mike	Cottell (Mick)	Pilot
Alastair	Crawford	Pilot
Peter	Davies (Junior)	Pilot
Ciaran	Denneny	Alice Springs Maintenance
Dina	Dennien	Katherine Office
Mark	Di Rosso	Pilot

TILLAIR-CHARTAIR STAFF 1977 - 1988

(Note surnames at time of employment are used)

Mark	Diamond (Diamo)	Pilot
Anne	Diepold	Katherine Office
Andrew	Downing	Pilot
Richard	Duldig (Slippery)	Pilot
Steven	Dyson	Pilot
Rory	Elston	Pilot
Geoff	English	Pilot
Wolfgang	Ertner	Katherine Office
Rosemary	Ey	Katherine Reservations
Barry	Foord	Accountant, Katherine Office
Shayne	George (Gecko)	Pilot
Cathy	Gleeson	Katherine Accounts
Maurie	Geue	Pilot
Milly	Goodings	Finance/Admin Manager
Walter	Gowans	Pilot
Paul	Grant (Spock)	Pilot
Mike	Green	
Grant	Gumley (GGG)	Pilot
Greg	Harris	Katherine Office
Cameron	Hartman (Pod)	Pilot
Brad	Hasket	Pilot
Andrew	Hockings (Lurch)	Pilot
Ron	Hoenger (Ronbo)	Engineer
Donna	Holland	Alice Springs Office
James	Hoskins	Pilot
Shirley	Hussie (Shirl)	Katherine Reservations
Max	Jamieson	Pilot
Brett	Jenson	Pilot
Mark	Jerdan (Jerdo)	Pilot
Graham	Johnstone	Pilot
David	Jones (DJ)	Pilot
Mark	Judson	Pilot
Dianne	Kelly	Brisbane office

TILLAIR-CHARTAIR STAFF 1977 - 1988
(Note surnames at time of employment are used)

Neil	Kerr	Pilot
David	Kienzle	Pilot
Ted	Landy	Pilot
Rosemary	Lincoln	Katherine Office
Ian	Lucas	Pilot
Mike	Lucas (Emil)	Pilot
Gerry	Luck	Katherine maintenance
Andrew	Maclean (Boggie)	Pilot
Kathy	Maloney	Alice Springs Office
Paul	Mann	Pilot
John	Marchant (Marcho)	Pilot
Tony	Markwell	Pilot
Dean	Marshall	Pilot
Tim	McCubbin (Muckagin)	Pilot
Tim	Metcalfe	Alice Springs maintenance
Simon	Milford (Mildew)	Pilot
Brett	Miller (Gibber)	Pilot
Barney	Milosev	Pilot
Jane	Mitchell	Travel agency
Mark	Morley	Pilot
Ken	Norman (Kenny Cool)	Pilot
Ian	Paige (Paigey)	Pilot
Stuart	Palframan	Pilot
David	Palmer	Pilot
Veronica	Peetz	Katherine Office
Bob	Petersen	Driver general duties
Joan	Petersen	Katherine reservations
Mike	Pitman	Ayers Rock refueller
Dave	Prior	Pilot
Neil	Prosser (Possum)	Pilot
Mark	Purdie	Pilot
Steve	Quilkey (Squilkey)	Pilot
Penny	Quinn	Katherine Accounts
Peter	Quinn (Quinny)	Pilot

TILLAIR-CHARTAIR STAFF 1977 - 1988
(Note surnames at time of employment are used)

Dave	Ramsay	Pilot
Gordon	Ramsay (Gundy)	Pilot
Mike	Rees (Reesy)	Pilot
Sean	Reynes	Pilot
Jenny	Richards	Katherine Office
Andrew	Ringwood (Ringers)	Pilot
Grahame	Roberts	Katherine maintenance
Brad	Rogers (Chronic)	Pilot
Ron	Rouse	Alice Springs maintenance
Brendon	Ryan	Aircraft engineer
Barry	Ryan (Bazza)	Pilot
Laurie	Shaw	Pilot
Sue	Sinclair	Katherine office
Pete	Stendall	Pilot
Noelene	Stevens	Katherine office
Peter	Stocks (SOMF)	Pilot
Mike	Strong (Dangles)	Pilot
Greg	Swain	Operations Manager, Katherine
Vicki	Thomas	Katherine office
Anne	Tickner	Katherine office
John	Torr (JT)	Pilot
Tim	Travers-Jones	Pilot
John	Trezona	Accountant
Keith	Tym	Pilot
Gary	Volkovickas	Alice Springs maintenance
Leigh	Ward	Katherine office
Peter	Wells (Legs)	Pilot
George	Westamacott	Pilot
Brian	Wilcox (Snoopy)	Pilot
Les	Wright	Pilot
Andrew	Youren (Slugger)	Pilot
Andrew	Zahn (Tug)	Pilot
Robert	Young	Pilot

FROM THE TILLAIR ALBUM

243

```
NEW VISION EVANGELICAL SOCIETY

nd Floor
V.A.I. Building
Gregory Terrace
Alice Springs
N.T. 5750

                                        Telephone: 522211

                                        24 October 1983

Tillair Air Charter,
Katherine Terrace,
Katherine,
NT 5780

For the Attention of:  Mr J. Torr

Dear Mr Torr,

Perhaps you have heard of me and my nationwide campaign
in the cause of temperance.  Each year for the past
fourteen, I have made a tour of Australia delivering a
series of lectures on the evils of drinking.

On these tours I have been accompanied by my young friend
and assistant, Clyde Linson.  Clyde, a young man of good
family and excellent background, is a pathetic example of
life ruined by excessive indulgence in whisky and women.
Clyde would appear with me at the lectures and sit on the
platform - drunk, wheezing, staring at the audience through
bleary and bloodshot eyes, sweating profusely, picking his
nose, belching and breaking wind and making obscene
gestures at the ladies, while I would point him out as an
example of what over indulgence can do to a person.

This summer, unfortunately, Clyde died.  A mutual friend
has given me your name and I wonder if you'd be available
to take Clyde's place on my 1983/84 tour.

Yours in evangelism,
```

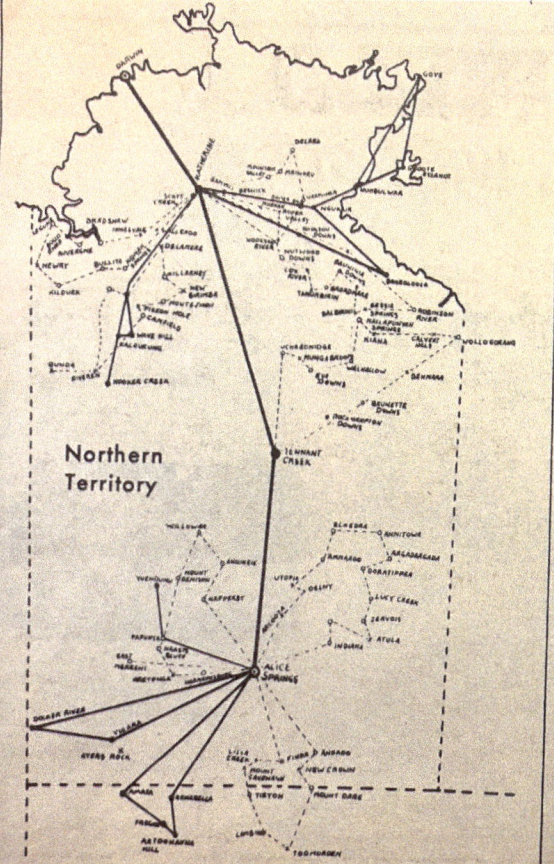

TILLAIR

RAILWAY ARCADE, KATHERINE TCE., P.O. BOX 1596
KATHERINE, N.T. 5780 TELEPHONE 72 1711 A.H. 72 1046
TELEX AA 85506

EFFECTIVE: 10th MARCH, 1984

ALICE SPRINGS TO TENNANT CREEK
Mon - Wed - Sat
Flight TL 174 C441

| ALICE SPRINGS | DEPART 1330 |
| TENNANT CREEK | ARRIVE 1450 |

TENNANT CREEK TO ALICE SPRINGS
Tues - Thurs - Sat - Sun
Flight TL 175 C441 Conquest

| TENNANT CREEK | DEPART 1100 |
| ALICE SPRINGS | ARRIVE 1220 |

ALICE SPRINGS — TENNANT — KATHERINE — DARWIN
Friday
Flight TL174 C441 Conquest

ALICE SPRINGS	DEPART 1330
TENNANT CREEK	ARRIVE 1450
	DEPART 1510
KATHERINE	ARRIVE 1640
	DEPART 1700
DARWIN	ARRIVE 1755

DARWIN—TENNANT—ALICE SPRINGS
Saturday
Flight TL 175 C441 Conquest

DARWIN	DEPART 0800
● TENNANT CREEK	ARRIVE 1020
	DEPART 1100
ALICE SPRINGS	ARRIVE 1220

● Optional call Katherine, Tillair Flights 174/175 meet and connect with TAA and Ansett Flights at Alice Springs.

AIR FARES

ALICE SPRINGS TO —
Tennant Creek	$101.80
Katherine	$222.50
Darwin	$299.20

TENNANT CREEK TO —
| Katherine | $120.70 |
| Darwin | $197.40 |

DARWIN TO —
| Katherine | $76.70 |

AIR CARGO RATES

ALICE SPRINGS TO —
Tennant Creek	$1.20 per kg
Katherine	$2.20 per kg
Darwin	$3.00 per kg

TENNANT CREEK TO —
| Katherine | $1.30 per kg |
| Darwin | $2.00 per kg |

KATHERINE TO —
| Darwin | $0.80 per kg |

BASIC CHARGE PER CONSIGNMENT $10.

BOOKINGS AT **TILLAIR** OR YOUR LOCAL TRAVEL AGENT.

OUTBACK MAIL AND PASSENGER SERVICE — AIR CHARTER — SCENIC FLIGHTS

ACKNOWLEDGEMENTS

Thanks, of course, to John Tilley and family members Jenny, Kate, Sarah, Scott and Penny for their efforts in recalling stories and sourcing documents, photographs and dozens of contacts around Australia.

The support of the Territory's indigenous and non-indigenous communities, including cattle station families and traditional settlements were integral to this story and the airline's growth and success. It is for these communities' needs that outback carriers such as Tillair existed.

Huge thanks for giving up their time to share their memories go to Tillair pilots Gary Boxall, the late John Marchant, Peter Quinn, Mark Jerdan, Keith Tym, Barney Milosev, Mike Lucas, Ian Lucas, Mike Strong, Hugh Cohen, Shayne George, Mike Cottell, Tim Travers-Jones, Stuart Palframan, Peter Davies and Scott Builder. Other friends, family and colleagues who proved immeasurably helpful include Suzy Tilley, Val Dyer, Sue Browne, Milly Goodings, Rosemary and Terry Ey, Ron Hoenger, Shirley Avis, Cathy Cohen, Bryce Baud, Jane Eastburn, John Hardy, Roger Leach, Patricia Kenny, Stephen Marshall and Geoff Anderson.

The editing and proofreading of this story to keep certain parties out of gaol was helped immensely by the diligent work of Tim McCubbin, Gordon Ramsay, John Torr, Hugh Cohen and Lisa Macken.

www.ingramcontent.com/pod-product-compliance
Lightning Source LLC
Chambersburg PA
CBHW061804290426

44109CB00031B/2935